LITIGATION STORY

HOW TO SURVIVE AND THRIVE
THROUGH THE LITIGATION PROCESS

STEPHANIE COUSINS

Copyright © 2021 Stephanie Cousins.

All rights reserved. No part of this book may be used or reproduced by any means, graphic, electronic, or mechanical, including photocopying, recording, taping or by any information storage retrieval system without the written permission of the author except in the case of brief quotations embodied in critical articles and reviews.

WestBow Press books may be ordered through booksellers or by contacting:

WestBow Press
A Division of Thomas Nelson & Zondervan
1663 Liberty Drive
Bloomington, IN 47403
www.westbowpress.com
844-714-3454

Because of the dynamic nature of the Internet, any web addresses or links contained in this book may have changed since publication and may no longer be valid. The views expressed in this work are solely those of the author and do not necessarily reflect the views of the publisher, and the publisher hereby disclaims any responsibility for them.

Any people depicted in stock imagery provided by Getty Images are models, and such images are being used for illustrative purposes only. Certain stock imagery © Getty Images.

All Scripture quotations, unless otherwise indicated, are taken from the Holy Bible, New International Version®, NIV®. Copyright ©1973, 1978, 1984, 2011 by Biblica, Inc.® Used by permission of Zondervan. All rights reserved worldwide. www.zondervan.com The "NIV" and "New International Version" are trademarks registered in the United States Patent and Trademark Office by Biblica, Inc.®

Scripture quotations marked (ESV) are from The ESV® Bible (The Holy Bible, English Standard Version®), copyright © 2001 by Crossway, a publishing ministry of Good News Publishers. Used by permission. All rights reserved.

Scripture marked (KJV) taken from the King James Version of the Bible.

Scripture marked (NKJV) taken from the New King James Version®. Copyright © 1982 by Thomas Nelson. Used by permission. All rights reserved.

Scripture quotations taken from the (NASB®) New American Standard Bible®, Copyright © 1960, 1971, 1977, 1995, 2020 by The Lockman Foundation. Used by permission. All rights reserved. www.lockman.org

Scripture quotations marked (NLT) are taken from the Holy Bible, New Living Translation, copyright ©1996, 2004, 2015 by Tyndale House Foundation. Used by permission of Tyndale House Publishers, a Division of Tyndale House Ministries, Carol Stream, Illinois 60188. All rights reserved.

ISBN: 978-1-6642-3078-1 (sc)
ISBN: 978-1-6642-3077-4 (e)

Print information available on the last page.

WestBow Press rev. date: 04/29/2021

CONTENTS

Preface vii

Introduction ix

Chapter 1   To File or Not to File 1

Chapter 2   Wrong Place, Wrong Time 3

Chapter 3   The Smoke Has Cleared 5

Chapter 4   The First Step 9

Chapter 5   Are You Able? 12

Chapter 6   You Have a Choice in Your Future................... 16

Chapter 7   Moving Forward and Making the Right Choices........... 18

Chapter 8   Seeking Legal Counsel.................................... 23

Chapter 9   What Do I Do Now?...................................... 26

Chapter 10 Maintaining Peace while Moving Forward 32

Chapter 11 To Work or Not to Work?............................... 35

Chapter 12 The Waiting Game 43

Chapter 13 Testifying... 48

Chapter 14 Don't Let the System Drag You Down.......... 53

Chapter 15 Keep Living 62

Chapter 16 The Decision Is Yours.................................... 66

Chapter 17 What Does the Bible Say?................................74

Notes 81

PREFACE

The secret to living well in this world
is to never look for justice, and
never cease to give it.
—Leonard Ravenhill

The purpose of this short book is to equip and empower you to not only navigate through the process of a lawsuit or workers' compensation claim due to a personal injury or accident but to control the entire process, achieving your best results legally, physically, emotionally, and spiritually. During your litigation, you will be in charge of your case—not the legal system and not the attorneys. You are not just another client, just another case, and just another injured worker, and you are not a statistic. Your rights matter, and you matter.

Don't let your injury, pain, and suffering destroy your life. You can easily and quickly educate yourself enough to master your journey through the legal process, and this book will show you how. I have kept it simple, because even though the law is confusing and technical, the steps to walking through litigation peacefully and victoriously are simple. Even if you are midway through litigation or thankfully near the end, the truths and principles for a successful life outlined in this book will remain constant throughout your entire life.

I have loved my career as a freelance court reporter. It is really all I've ever wanted to do. I have had the opportunity to meet some of the finest people on earth, and it has been a genuine blessing of a lifetime. I guess at the end of my day and the end of my career, I feel honored to be a part of justice that got done.

INTRODUCTION

Being a court reporter has given me the rare and precious privilege of being allowed to enter into other people's suffering at their most personal level, where a sudden trauma has occurred, and their lives have been turned upside down. Because a court reporter remains silent throughout all proceedings and has no vested interest in the matter, I've made it a personal endeavor to listen carefully, observe, and study not only the people who are testifying but the reactions of other people in the room as well.

When you have nothing to do but mindlessly pound on a keyboard, your mind is very tuned in to what people are saying, what they're not saying, their body posture, facial expressions, what they do when they're lying or faking, what rocks their emotions, what makes them angry, what incites their passion, how they feel about themselves, what kind of faith they have or don't have, and the list goes on.

My name is Amicus Curiae. As a Friend of the Court, it is my aim to help you through this difficult life challenge you are facing and carry you through to the end, where you break free from any and all aftermath of your accident or injury, *healed and whole*, maybe even better than you were before your trauma.

So if the Son sets you free, you will be free indeed.
—John 8:36, approximately AD 30

CHAPTER 1

To File or Not to File

*Discourage litigation. Persuade your neighbors to compromise
whenever you can. Point out to them how the nominal winner
is often a real loser—in fees, expenses, and waste of time.*
—Abraham Lincoln[1]

"Do you solemnly swear or affirm that the testimony you are about to
give will be the truth, the whole truth, and nothing but the truth?"
As the witness answered in the affirmative, it was quite evident
to me, from personal observation in the parking lot and unintended
overhearing in the reception area, that over the course of the next three-
plus hours of deposition testimony, this woman had her own version of
the truth and would say and do whatever it took to convince everyone in
the room that she was a poor, helpless victim who deserved justice—and
a hefty check—to compensate her for all that she had lost:

1. The ability to function normally, both physically and emotionally,
   without pain
2. The ability to work and earn money
3. The ability to have fun and enjoy life
4. Hope for the future

For thirty-seven years, I have been a participant of thousands of
depositions serving as a freelance court reporter. You know, that bored-
looking woman who sits like a statue at this tiny typewriter-like thing

Stephanie Cousins

called a steno machine, magically turning every word spoken in the room into a beautiful, expensive book called a *Transcript*. That's me.

The short definition of a court reporter is a person whose occupation is to transcribe the spoken word into written form using a shorthand machine to produce official transcripts of court hearings, depositions, and other official proceedings. Maybe you have seen one in action on TV, or maybe you have had the nerve-racking privilege of testifying yourself with a court reporter present, writing down your every word.

Over the course of the past three and a half decades, I am happy to say that only once have I been on the other side of the table, giving a deposition. I felt the pressure of all eyes on me, my so-called adversary waiting for me to stumble over an answer—or worse yet, in my uneasy chair, answer incorrectly out of forgetfulness or nervousness, which may have given the impression I was trying to lie or deceive.

Of course, there are always the following hours, days, and maybe months afterward where you retrace your every word and wish you would have answered differently; you feel embarrassed about how petty your accuser made you feel in that room; you realize that you omitted certain dimensions of your suffering to save yourself the embarrassment and humiliation, and you remember all the important aspects of your case that you neglected to bring up because you just wanted to get out of there as fast as you could!

For some personality types, just the thought of having all eyes on them while testifying in front of attorneys or a judge and/or a jury can cause enough fear to discourage them from filing a claim or a lawsuit, causing cancellation of recovery to which they are entitled.

For other personalities, the attitude looks more like "Those guys are gonna pay for what they did to me!" causing irrational thinking, emotional turmoil, and disastrous actions that cannot be undone.

Still other types of people are pleased to just have their medical expenses, car expenses, and lost wages paid, hoping to just get it over with as soon as possible, thinking, *I don't want to cause any trouble*, resulting in agreements and settlements far below what they deserve.

Are you one of these personality types, or are you somewhere in between?

Lawsuits can be time-consuming, stressful, and expensive, and no one knows what the end result will be when it's all said and done. You must take careful consideration before leaping into one.

CHAPTER 2

Wrong Place, Wrong Time

"Oh, if I would have just left the house five seconds
earlier, I would have never been in this accident."

"If I'd only went to see the plant nurse sooner when I
first started hurting, I could have avoided all of this
investigation, but I thought it was just a strain."

Don't be so hard on yourself. As the old saying goes, accidents do
happen, no matter who you are and regardless of how cautious you
are. Very seldom after an accident or injury do we immediately know
the full extent of what has happened to us physically and emotionally.
Often, the onset of pain takes a little time to kick in, and we can vigorously
try to convince ourselves that it will go away with a little rest or ice. But
sometimes rest is just not enough, and we are left with real problems: pain,
strain, sprain, broken bones, nightmares—trauma. It can be extremely
difficult to know where to start with the insurance process and even harder
to maneuver through all the requirements of our insurance companies or
our employers: who to report an injury to, how to report an injury, how to
get the medical attention you need, and so on. You can take a deep breath
and relax, because this book will guide you all the way.

Most people believe that insurance companies will do everything
they can to deny coverage for a claim or pay out as little as possible.
After all, they are in the business to make money, right? Unless you
have been through the process before, it is impossible to know all the
right steps to take when you've been injured unless you are prepared and

Stephanie Cousins

equipped. But you can have all the knowledge and skills necessary to face insurance companies and lawyers without insurance training or a law degree. Knowledge is power, and knowing more will very rapidly boost your confidence and success after an injury or trauma and enable you to walk through the process necessary in order to handle what lies ahead with great courage and hope.

CHAPTER 3

The Smoke Has Cleared

Warning: At this time, take control over your conversations and your signature. Do not say or sign anything that you may later regret.

The smoke has cleared, and you are now home from the hospital, emergency room, or scene of your accident or injury. You are probably tired, experiencing some pain, and quite possibly weak and vulnerable right now. It has been a whirlwind. I am so glad you found this book. Taking care of yourself should be your number one priority. Your injuries and emotional health are more important than anything right now.

People who are injured frequently say it was one of the worst days of their life, and I believe it. Why do bad things happen to good people? Often, we are just living, working, and doing life the best we can—and right out of nowhere we suffer an injury that seems to alter the course of our lives. But right where you are, right where you stand, you can and must move forward with diligence and purpose.

Please do not let anyone at this time pressure you to do or say or sign anything. Police officers and insurance agents often come at us too fast, and it is easy to feel threatened or intimidated into making a quick statement or signing a document that you later regret. Sad to say it, but it is very common for insurance adjusters to try to get you to sign away your rights quickly under the guise of helping you. No good and solid decisions are made in haste, and this is your life. Take control over your conversations and your signature!

Please also bear in mind from this point forward that you should do your best to document your injuries/accident. Keep together in a folder all

5

medical records, accident reports, photographs, witness statements, and contact information you have accumulated. If you or someone on your behalf can, take photographs of the accident scene and your bodily injuries as soon as possible. As today's new mantra goes, "If it wasn't documented, it didn't happen." Professionals love to use and misuse this saying, so be on top of it.

Get as much information together as you can as soon as possible because evidence gets lost and memories and recollections fade over time. Somehow, you have gotten your hands on this book, and that is not by mere chance. Now take control and relax—yes, these two things can be done at the same time!

Speaking to an insurance adjuster without knowing what to do or say can be a costly mistake. Remember, they have a job to do. I have many friends who work for insurance companies, and they are good and honest people. But not all adjusters are our friends, even though they may try to earn that position of trust with you, and you would be wise to get your comfort and compassion elsewhere. I would never give a written or recorded statement before seeking counsel. When you must talk with an insurance agent, be polite, of course, but stand firm in your dealings with them and let your conversation be short and to the point. Even though you may feel panicked about medical bills or the need to get your car fixed, unfortunately, you may also have injuries or damages that you are not aware of yet.

It is never a good time to make important decisions when you are under stress. So do not let the insurance company, or your employer, pressure you. You need to take your time and determine whether you need to consult with a lawyer. Insurance companies will take a claim much more seriously when a lawyer is involved. So many people forfeit what they are legally entitled to because of lack of knowledge. Let's face it: so much of this legal stuff is over our heads, and this is probably a brand-new experience for you. Yes, we learn from experience, but it does not have to be *your* experience.

It is important to know that you are entitled to your feelings right now, and nobody should try and tell you what's "normal." You are the one that is hurting, and the very fact that you are reading this proves that you

Litigation Story

are strong and courageous, despite pain and suffering. No one else needs to validate you, and you do not have to prove that you are "legitimate."

Here are just a few of the different emotions and feelings that people deal with postaccident and postinjury. Common, but not experienced by all, and all totally normal: shock, denial or disbelief, feeling numb, confused, helpless, afraid, shame, humiliation, self-blame, bouts of anger, irritability, unpredictable mood swings, sadness or crying, difficulty concentrating, unable to relax or sleep, nightmares, loss of appetite, feeling unsociable, and having no energy.

Despite what just happened to you, life goes on. The demands of work, marriage, children, school, daily grooming, daily chores, appointments, bill paying, and so on, continue right where you left off. What do you do?

> Whether you choose to move on from your struggles and
> enjoy life or waddle in your misery, life will continue.
> —Germany Kent[1]

Take a deep breath. The world did not end, and you are still alive. Please resist that powerful urge to throw a little pity party for yourself. There is no time for that. You have too many things to do and so much to accomplish in this life. You are not a victim, even if you "feel" like one. Do not trust your feelings right now. Feelings are fleeting and can change by the hour. Pity cannot heal your pain. Pity cannot pay your bills. And pity cannot fix your damaged car.

Use everything you can muster up inside to avoid the temptation of feeling sorry for yourself. What happened to you stinks, but you are still alive!

This may be the perfect time for you to sit or lie down in a quiet place and make a list of all the incredibly wonderful benefits of life you've been given, most of which we daily take for granted. Have you ever thought about how many accidents you were not involved in because you missed it by a split second? Seriously, there are so many times we are not injured when we should have been. You may be going through one of the worst times of your life, but you are greatly blessed in so many ways.

Are you blessed? You be the judge.

Twenty-one thousand people die every day from hunger or malnutrition.

Stephanie Cousins

An estimated 1.6 billion, more than 20 percent of the world's population, lack adequate housing.

The average distance that someone in a developing community walks to fetch water is 3.75 miles. Every twenty-one seconds a child dies of water-related disease.

An estimated 801,000 children younger than five years of age perish from diarrhea each year. This amounts to 11 percent of the 7.6 million deaths of children under the age of five and means that about twenty-two hundred children are dying every day as a result of diarrheal diseases.

Out of more than seven billion people on earth, more than twenty-five million are in forced labor.

There are forty million adults and children in forced labor and sexual slavery.

Throughout the world, an estimated 2.4 billion people lack basic sanitation (more than 32 percent of the world's population).

Twenty percent of the world's population (1.4 billion people) lives on less than $1.25 a day.

Fourteen percent of the world's population cannot read.

One in three children in the world—230 million under the age of five—do not have a birth certificate, effectively cutting them off from accessing life-saving health care and other critical services.

We truly have so much to be thankful for, and the evidence of blessings exist everywhere. Your situation could be worse. As they say, if we threw our problems in a pile and saw everyone else's, we'd grab our own back. Being a thankful person is a choice only you can make that will enable you to successfully handle daily stress and improve your life radically.

CHAPTER 4

The First Step

You are at the very precipice of making a decision that may well affect you for the rest of your life. Take control over your situation. Do not let your situation take control over you.

Step 1. Decide that no matter what has happened to you, you are going to make it through, and you will not allow this injury/accident to destroy your life or your happiness. We call this intentional living. Do not let this situation control you, but you control it. I cannot stress enough how important your attitude is standing where you are right now.

It is extremely vital that you accept what happened *to* you and decide immediately that it will not become a part *of* you. In other words, not letting it become a part of who you are. Yes, you may have an injured back, neck, knee, shoulder, or all the above, but on the inside, you are still the same person.

Understand that you are not your injury. What I mean is, I am still Steve. I am not Steve with a broken back. Never describe yourself by the injury or pain with which you live. The more you personalize pain or an injury, the more power you give to it. Do not call it "my pain" or "my accident." Why feed the monster?

Police yourself and the words that you say. What you tell yourself matters. Put to death any negative self-talk. Try to purge the words *never* and *always* from your vocabulary, and do not be self-cursed:

"I will never again be able to …"

"I'll always feel like …"

"I'll never have the strength to …"

9

Stephanie Cousins

"My life will never be …"

> Death and life are in the power of the tongue. (Proverbs
> 18:21 ESV; King Solomon)

Do you identify yourself around your medical problem? Are you making it a part of who you are? My bad back, my arthritis, my bad heart, my fibromyalgia? (You would not believe the number of people who get labeled with fibromyalgia after an accident. It can be a very debilitating condition that is often hard to diagnose.) Are you saying my headaches, my inability to sleep, my ruined life?

People are often quick in deciding a condition or a situation is their "new normal." Often, the reason is that while they are intentionally thinking about their injury and all the damage it has caused, it becomes a part of their everyday life. It becomes their natural default. Trauma is a horrible thing, but it does not have to consume you or become your identity. Our injuries are not the definition of our lives!

It is so easy after an injury to begin feeling sorry for yourself and complaining. I understand. You have experienced something awful. But don't stay there long feeling sorry for yourself because this posture will get you nowhere and drive others away.

"To complain" in the old Hebrew is *luwn*, which literally means to lodge or spend the night. In other words, when we complain, we will reside there, or lodge there for a while, usually all night and into the next morning. Then how miserable and unhappy we feel, as do the poor souls around us that have to listen to it.

And please do not waste your time wondering, *Why me?* I think the question we should be asking ourselves is, "Why not me?"

For instance, I drive approximately thirty thousand miles per year and have only been involved in two car accidents. According to the National Highway Traffic Safety Administration, there are more than six million police-reported motor vehicle accidents in the United States every year.[1] I have been very fortunate.

I thank God that I have never been injured at work, and I'm very sorry if you have been. According to the National Safety Council, we have approximately 510 work injuries per hour, 12,600 per day, and 88,500 per

Litigation Story

week, which equates to around 4.6 million work injuries per year in the United States.[2]

You may be asking, "Why did this happen to me? Why is God allowing this suffering in my life, and what kind of a God would let this happen to me?" Bad things do happen to good people. The Bible says that it rains on the just and the unjust. Everyone has negative experiences in this life, and you were given this one, just like millions of other people around the world were given theirs. But you and you alone make the choice whether to live life positively or to wallow in self-pity and misery. You can have an ugly and bitter experience following your accident or injury, or you can determine to deal with your situation the best way possible, growing as a person as you rebound with a victory! What's it gonna be?

Unforgiveness and anger will cause you additional suffering and prevent you from moving on, and you absolutely must keep yourself from self-pity or trying to extract pity or sympathy from others. I would tell you right now, if you are an individual who lives and thrives on attention-seeking, pity, and sympathy *and are unwilling to change,* you can just throw this book away immediately. This book is not for you. This book is for those of us who want to live life to the fullest, to live a life that counts for something, to be an asset to society and not just a "taker."

Let's face it. It's depressing to be around people who are just existing, but it's a blast to hang around those that believe there is a purpose for their life and that live intentionally and with passion. Trauma is not a life sentence, and you will get through this. Your attitude and purposeful mindset at this time will set the course of your future.

11

CHAPTER 5

Are You Able?

*I was never ruined but twice; once when I lost
a lawsuit and once when I won one.*
—Voltaire (1694–1778)[1]

If you are still reading, you are a prime candidate to work through a claim/litigation successfully, with your head held high, because you still have

1. the *ability* to function, both physically and emotionally;
2. the *ability* to have fun and enjoy life;
3. the *ability* to do some form of work and earn money (most, but not all); and
4. the *ability* to maintain or grasp hope for the future.

How do I know that you still possess these precious things? Because you are reading! Of course, there are exceptions, and I seriously pray that is not you. I have personally met people who seemed to have lost everything, and I am quite certain you have met them too. It is unbelievable and heartbreaking to listen to their stories. Many times, after I have reported their testimony, I have tried to block it from my mind because it was so painful to listen to. There are kind and caring lawyers who will offer Kleenex and ask the witness if they would like to take a recess, and there are also seemingly cold and unattached lawyers whose agenda is all that matters, who just keep right on asking tough questions during the sobs and tears.

Litigation Story

Some people have experienced multiple, devastating, and life-altering injuries: paralysis from the waist down, waking up in the hospital and discovering their right leg had been amputated, spinal cord injuries, disfigurement, multiple operations, setbacks, failures and infections with prosthetics, total inability to work, impotency, the abandonment of a spouse that couldn't cope with the tragedy and all the changes that came with it, struggles with depression, people so desperate that they try to take their own lives.

It is impossible to even comprehend the magnitude of what they have been through, and we should never say to someone, "I know exactly what you're going through." Because we don't. The saddest part to the stories is that while there are multitudes of individuals who consider that they were given a second chance at life and go on to living amazing lives and impact the world with what they've learned, there are also multitudes of people who never go down that path and, therefore, their loss is horrific and completely devastating. I really hope this is not you.

I have reported countless testimonies of people who have suffered an accident or injury—hundreds and hundreds. While the list of the life-changing damage it has caused varies in degree, for the most part, the testimony is basically the same. Having said that, I must also tell you that I have only encountered a handful of people testifying who lack the *ability* to physically function to some degree, the *ability* to have fun and enjoy life, the *ability* to work in some capacity and earn money, or the *ability* to grasp hope for the future, but they cannot push through because they have become paralyzed by their circumstances. Perhaps a better way to say it is that they have allowed their circumstances to paralyze them.

Ability is the key word. You have the ability, but will you exercise it? Are you going to let this accident/injury ruin your life, or will you try with all your power to hold on to what you possess in life—your relationship with your spouse, your children, your friends, your job, your leisure, and your hope? Only you can make that critical decision.

Do not allow yourself to become paralyzed, stuck in neutral. This is worth repeating: Do not put your life in neutral! It's tempting to say, "When I get on the other side of this thing, then I will start over." It rarely happens because thinking patterns and habits have already taken root. Neutral gear has become a trap.

Stephanie Cousins

Oh, the countless irreplaceable individuals I have met who are stuck in neutral. I'm telling you, hopelessness and depression appear to be at an all-time high. People I encounter are scared, angry and desperate, going through the motions of life and struggling just to get through another day. This does not have to be *your* position! You will not be taken captive and imprisoned by a personal injury or accident that has thrust you into the court system. You are being empowered and educated through this book to proceed forward with boldness before that very system chews you up and spits you out.

Right now, make up your mind. Are you going to let your accident, your injury, or the harm that has been done to you destroy you and destroy your life, your marriage, your family, your desire to earn a buck and be a part of society, or the enjoyment that life can give you? We are only given one life to live here on this earth. What are you going to do with it?

> Nothing in this world is worth having or worth
> doing unless it means effort, pain, difficulty.
> —Theodore Roosevelt[2]

You don't get in life what you want. You get what you fight for. Nothing worth having comes easy. If you cannot bring yourself to the right *attitude* and consciously make a decision that you will not let destruction come upon you and your household … well, again, we've come to a point in this book where you can throw it away. Attitude matters. It has been said, and is true, that your attitude will determine your altitude. Martin Seligman, called the "Father of Positive Psychology" and the author of several bestselling books, found that negative people get sick more often, are divorced more frequently, and raise kids who get in more trouble. Dr. Seligman even found that negative people make less money.[3]

> Most people are about as happy as they make up their minds to be.
> —Abraham Lincoln[4]

Seriously, please take your time in making the decision. Because not only will your life be dramatically impacted but also the lives of everyone around you and those you love. Do not make a permanent decision for your

Litigation Story

temporary emotions. We always regret emotional decisions or decisions we make in a hurry, when we are scared, or when we are at our weakest.

Your life is the sum total of the decisions you make every day. You will be OK if you say yes to proceeding with a claim; and you will be OK if you say no to proceeding with a claim. It is indecision that drains the joy out of life. Yes and no are the most powerful words you will ever say. You need to be able to say them with precision because they will determine your destiny. You alone possess the power to make a mind-blowing comeback from your accident or injury; and conversely, you also have the power to allow your accident or injury to result in an irreversible and self-destructing spiral down toward horrific and devastating loss.

Do you want to be that person that makes a mind-blowing comeback? Then buckle up and keep reading. Take some more deep breaths and relax. You're going to be fine.

CHAPTER 6

You Have a Choice in Your Future

Avoid lawsuits beyond all things; they pervert your conscience,
impair your health and dissipate your property.
—Jean de la Bruyere[1]

According to the *Harvard Business Review*[2], more than 90 percent of all lawsuits are settled out of court, most of them virtually on the courthouse steps after months or years of preparation and expense. We have all heard stories of long, painful, drawn-out lawsuits and shocking verdicts—some we have applauded and some with which we've been disgusted. A formal legal proceeding can take a toll in many different ways.

Step 2. If you are still reading, I commend you for trying to help yourself. I believe you have made a wise decision. So many people consider themselves just a victim of circumstance. You are not a victim of circumstance. You have a choice in your future, and life is not passive (definition of passive: not acting to influence or change a situation; allowing other people to be in control). Your next move is to decide if litigation is something you want to pursue.

Repeatedly, I've listened to the personal heartbreaking stories of good, honest, hard-working people whose lives have been shattered as a result of an accident or personal injury, followed by pending litigation that exponentially compounded their heartache and trouble. But this does not have to happen to you! You are not just a statistic.

I couldn't even begin to count the number of times I've heard people say, "This has been dragging on forever," or "I don't even remember what

Litigation Story

life was like before all this started," or "I feel like my whole life has been put on hold."

Do you have what it takes to survive the legal system? Do you have the emotional wherewithal? Do you have a support system surrounding you and will they support the decision you make regarding filing suit or making a claim, even if they do not agree with what you're doing? Do you feel like you personally need that approval, acceptance, and support of your spouse, family, or others to proceed with litigation? Do you have enough money if you need to pay for a lawyer and legal expenses?

In other words, is it worth it, or is it necessary?

Only you can answer these important questions. We have all heard stories of where litigation pursuit did more harm than good. Please take your time in deciding. Do not let anyone persuade you or rush you into your decision. At the end of the day, it is your decision, and you will have to live with it.

CHAPTER 7

Moving Forward and Making
the Right Choices

"I can't help the way I feel." Is that true?

tep 3. If you have decided to move forward with an attorney, many personal choices that you can make before you do contact an attorney will equip you immediately. These are a few of the most important *active* choices that I believe you can make:

a. The choice to control your thoughts. Most people by nature have negative and toxic thinking, and it does not have to be that way. You *can* control your thoughts. A massive amount of helpful information is out there addressing this subject.

Please, if you have a negative mouth, *stop it*! Don't be lazy; attack this life-destroyer. Negative and toxic thinking and speaking affects everything about us: our emotions, our health, our jobs, our relationships—yes, everything!

According to a leading financial whiz, we produce up to fifty thousand thoughts a day, and 70 percent to 80 percent of those thoughts are negative. And some research suggests we speak at about two hundred words per minute, but we can listen to and process thirteen hundred words per minute.

As a court reporter, I can tell you that most people speak at about two hundred words per minute, with gusts up to four hundred.

Take charge of your thoughts and speech; quit saying negative things about yourself and others. Nobody likes to be around that. Stop it! Positive

Litigation Story

thinking doesn't just happen. You must make it happen. A man in my community is called "Dark Cloud" because when you get around him, the atmosphere is going to change. The environment is going to shift from a positive force to a negative force in record-breaking time. I'm quite certain we have all experienced Dark Clouds. They can zap the life right out of you and bring your mood down in an instant. Monitor what you take in and what you put out.

b. Moving forward, in addition to possessing the power to control your thoughts, you have the choice to forgive whoever has hurt you. No, you don't have to tell them that you forgive them (although, it has been proven to be extremely helpful), but purposefully, out loud, and whenever you think about it say, "I forgive _____ for _____." Spill your guts to yourself and out loud! It is very therapeutic.

Deal with any anger issues you may have swiftly, whether it is an individual or a company that caused you harm, so you do not become hateful, pessimistic, bitter, and miserable to be around. If you do not choose to practice forgiveness in your personal life, everyone you come into contact with will suffer, and you will be the one who pays most dearly.

You and you alone will make the choice: Do I hold on to anger, resentment, and maybe even thoughts of revenge, or do I choose to forgive, which will take me down the path of emotional, physical, and spiritual health? You are only one decision away from freedom—the decision to forgive.

Let's face it. We have all been hurt by words and actions of others when we didn't deserve it. Get over it! Please free yourself from the role of victim. You, too, have done and said things to others who did not deserve it. No matter how you feel, get up, dress up, show up, and be an awesome you. You have greater power than how you *feel*. You will get through this!

It's not what happens to you, but how you react to it that matters.
—Epictetus, AD 55–135[1]

It is your decision and your decision alone. Do you want to be a prisoner of the one who hurt you, or do you want to let go and be free and in control of your feelings, your attitudes, and your life?

19

Stephanie Cousins

Unforgiveness is like a disease, and according to Dr. Steven Standiford, chief of surgery at the Cancer Treatment Centers of America, refusing to forgive makes people sick and keeps them that way.[2]

According to experts at John Hopkins Hospital, studies have found that the act of forgiveness can reap huge rewards for your health—lowering the risk of heart attack; improving cholesterol levels and sleep; and reducing pain, blood pressure, and levels of anxiety, depression, and stress. And research points to an increase in the forgiveness-health connection as you age.[3]

Karen Swartz, MD, director of the Mood Disorders Adult Consultation Clinic at Johns Hopkins Hospital, has said this about forgiveness:

> Forgiveness is not just about saying the words. It is an active process in which you make a *conscious decision* to let go of negative feelings whether the person deserves it or not.[4]

This very act will make you free of becoming bitter and resentful and mean, imprisoned by the one who harmed you. Right feelings follow right actions, and that action is forgiving. Forgiveness brings a kind of peace that helps you go on with life, instead of nursing a "poor me" mentality.

> Hanging on to resentment is letting someone
> you despise live rent-free in your head.
> —Ann Landers[5]

c. Not only can you actively choose to control your thinking daily and forgive those who harmed you, but you must also make the choice to keep moving. Do not let your life stagnate, do not let yourself waste away, and do not allow yourself to be mentally and/or physically paralyzed by your current situation.

Take some advice from some of the earth's oldest living Guinness World Record holders:

Bob Weighton, 112, of Britain: "I just take life as it comes along."

Gertrude Weaver, 116, of Arkansas: "Treat people right and be nice to other people the way you want them to be nice to you."

Besse Berry Cooper-Brown, 116, of Georgia: "One of the secrets to living so long is staying out of others' business."

Chitetsu Watanabe, 113, of Japan: The secret to longevity is not to get angry and keep a smile on your face."

Jeanne Calment, 122, of France: "Always keep your smile. That's how I explain my long life."

You must keep moving forward with your life and with your body! This cannot be emphasized enough. If you don't keep moving, it's so easy to get trapped in the house, paralyzed in your own little world. This is a miserable mistake, and you will pay a high price for it.

Even though it is very normal after an injury/accident to want to just stay in bed and let life pass you by for a while, please don't do it! You are in a very fragile and volatile position at this time, and your decision to keep moving is critical to your recovery and well-being.

> Pain doesn't tell you when you ought to stop. Pain is
> the little voice in your head that tries to hold you back
> because it knows if you continue, you will change.
> —Kobe Bryant[6]

Yes, follow your doctor's instructions, if you trust him or her, and move that body as much as you are able. Do that very "thing" that you don't want to do, like get out of bed, take a bath, stretch or exercise, do some cooking or cleaning, regardless of how minimal it seems. Go outdoors if possible and get some clean, fresh air, and do not refuse social activities unless you absolutely must. You do not have to *feel* like going out in order to go out and have a great time.

Care for yourself the very best you can. Do your own research and educate yourself to discover what works for you, what makes you stronger, and what makes you feel better. Be your own advocate. Knowledge is power!

d. Not only do you have to keep moving forward and choose to control your thoughts and choose to forgive whoever has hurt you; you have to make the choice and intentionally decide now that you will not let a claim/lawsuit, or its outcome, control your life. Make up your mind that you

Stephanie Cousins

will only think about it, work on it, or talk about it when necessary. It is not *a part of you*. It is only *a matter that involves you* that will be resolved.

It hurts to say it or think it, but prepare yourself for losing a case, just in case, or receiving an outcome that you were not expecting. Being victorious does not necessarily mean that you win your case. But victory can mean that you have overcome a trauma and walked through the ramifications of that trauma victoriously, healed and made whole, with your head held high, which is truly something of which to be proud.

Determine in advance that you will be OK regardless of whether you win or lose a potential claim. Life will go on with or without your participation, but you will only live this life once. Make the most of it! Decide and proclaim that you are going to heal and live an exciting and wonderful life no matter what. It may be impossible for you to understand why you must go through what you are going through. We live life forward, but only understand it backward.

Keep reading. Your story is going to have a happy ending, whether you win or lose your case.

CHAPTER 8

Seeking Legal Counsel

A man who is his own lawyer has a fool for a client.

tep 4. If you have chosen to simply consult with an attorney or you have already decided to retain one, here we go! Hold your head up high because you are smarter than you give yourself credit for. You are strong and capable to make decisions for yourself, and do not let any preconceived attitudes about lawyers turn you toward skepticism, fear, feelings of inferiority, or worries about not being smart enough to have a meeting with them. I may be a professional court reporter, but I am also a farmer, and I believe my "simple" upbringing and living is the truly intelligent part of me!

You are learning not only how to navigate through your case, but how to be in control of it—how to be represented.

I would highly encourage a decision not to take on the system by yourself. Even experienced lawyers typically do not represent themselves in court. You wouldn't try to set your own broken leg in order to save money or to avoid the medical field, and you would never drill and fill your own teeth, would you?

If you do seek legal counsel, be honest with them. Most lawyers offer a free consultation to hear your story. If you do not like him or her, for any reason, go somewhere else. There is no reason to work with someone who isn't a good listener or who doesn't value your time or appreciate your particular accident or injury.

The mission of the American Association for Justice is to promote a fair and effective justice system—and to support the work of attorneys in

23

Stephanie Cousins

their efforts to ensure that any person who is injured by the misconduct or negligence of others can obtain justice in America's courtrooms, even when taking on the most powerful interests.[1]

I have had the amazing privilege of working with some of the finest lawyers in America, many of whom I can call friend. Consequently, as a result of working with hundreds of *good ones* throughout my career, here are a few warning signs of the *not so good ones* that I've observed or heard stories about:

- Not returning your calls or emails.
- Having little consideration for your time.
- Falls asleep, plays on phone, misses appointments, or shows up late.
- No compassion or understanding.
- Lack of enthusiasm/seems unsure about your case.
- Unclear billing, hidden expenses. A good lawyer is transparent about his or her fees.
- Lack of decisiveness or clear-cut plan.
- Not having documents filed by the deadline, filing the wrong paperwork, or filing paperwork incorrectly.
- Making important decisions without asking you first.
- Lack of communication about your case.
- Unethical/illegal behavior.
- Speaks to you in a condescending way, or other signs of disrespect.

Do not be afraid to ask questions. You are not only paying a lawyer to help you with a case but to communicate and give you his or her best service. The lawyer is representing you, and it is your body. If you feel your attorney is not attentive to your case and getting back to you in a timely manner, if your attorney doesn't give you status updates and is not clearly communicating his or her progress, if you are not receiving copies of important lawsuit correspondence—legal, medical, or otherwise—or if you are rarely having dialogue, you need to find out why.

Try to sit down and ask your attorney why: "Is there any reason I should have to wait for information, updates, or timely communications of consequential information?" If you are not satisfied with the answer,

Litigation Story

get another attorney. It will save you time and money if you establish your satisfaction or dissatisfaction with your attorney's conduct as early as possible—right from the word *go*.

No Good Question Goes Unbilled

A man went to a lawyer and asked, "What is your fee?"
"It's $100 for three questions," answered the lawyer.
"Isn't that a little steep?" said the man.
"Yes," said the lawyer. "Now, what's your third question?"

The American Bar Association reported in August 2019 that there were 1,352,027 licensed attorneys in the United States.[2] It is important to do your research when selecting a lawyer, and a referral from someone you know and respect may be your best source. There are good and caring attorneys out there. I know. I work with them daily. Make sure *you* get yourself a good one!

A jury consists of twelve persons chosen to
decide who has the better lawyer.
—Robert Frost[3]

Take your place, stand your ground, and run your case. Do not let your case run you!

CHAPTER 9

What Do I Do Now?

You took that giant step and spoke with a lawyer. Now what?

Step 5. Do all the legwork and paperwork your attorney has given you to do diligently and truthfully. It is extraordinarily helpful to begin journaling a chronology of your life: your pain and symptoms, your medical treatment, the limitations of your activities due to pain and injury, and other necessary information, for future reference. Most attorneys will request you prepare this document for them. Yes, it can be time-consuming and annoying, trying to remember and document everything, but it is necessary and will prove to be unbelievably valuable to you.

I am quite certain that even though the events surrounding your accident or injury may have been one of the worst times of your life, as the days, weeks, months, and years pass, the details start to get fuzzy. Trauma can do that to you, and experts say this is normal and healthy. Some things are not meant to be remembered, and you do not have to apologize for being human. Witnesses during depositions are always amazed (and aggravated) when being asked to recall events and dates from the past. And who could blame them? I mean, who remembers this stuff?

"Q. What did Dr. Smith tell you about your restrictions on August 3, 2014?
A. Uh—

Litigation Story

Q. How many times in the previous winter did you have occasion to walk in that parking lot?
A. Are you kidding me?

Q. What did you tell your supervisor when he came to see you in the hospital after your accident and you were, according to your testimony, on morphine and "out of it"?
A. How could I possibly know that? I was out of it!

Q. What was the reason you called in sick to work on December 22, 2015?
A. Seriously? You expect me to remember that?

Q. How many times did you shovel snow the winter prior to your injury?
A. I—

Q. After your surgery, what was your pain level on May 17, 2017, on a scale of one to ten?
A. I couldn't possibly remember, but you're making my pain a ninety-nine on the one-to-ten scale right now!

Q. How many times had you had occasion to stop at that traffic light prior to your accident?
A. Uh, every time I stopped.

Q. Why did you post on Facebook on September 7, 2016, that you had the best vacation ever?
A. If you tell me where I went on vacation, maybe I can remember.

Q. When you entered that store on July 10, the date of your slip-and-fall, what shoes were you wearing, how long had you had them, what kind of tread did they have, what color were they, where did you buy them, what condition were they in, and where are they now?"

Exactly! Keep a journal!
Here is a great list of things to keep track of for future reference:

Stephanie Cousins

- Prescribed medications, dosages, and side effects
- Over-the-counter medicine expenses
- Time off work and lost pay
- Mileage to and from appointments with health-care providers (such as doctors, chiropractors, and physical therapists)
- Medical bills and records from health-care providers and insurance company related to your care and medical expenses
- Expenses for help with housework/yard work that you can no longer perform
- Mechanic work you can no longer perform
- All correspondence with work related to accident and injuries
- All correspondence with insurance
- Time and expenses for nursing care provided by professionals, friends, or family
- Emails, text messages, or other correspondence from witnesses or other people with knowledge of your injuries or accident and their contact information
- All correspondence with attorney
- Photographs pertaining to accident and injuries
- Pain journaling and journaling of limitations of activities, inability to sleep, and so forth

Don't include in your journal things that are not related to your case, and do not make entries that would prove to be embarrassing to you in the event your journal ends up in someone else's hands (because it probably will).

During a deposition, a witness will most likely be asked questions regarding activities of daily living, indoor/outdoor activities, and so much more, in order to determine how one's life has truly been affected by an accident or injury. Activities most commonly inquired about, from my experience, include such things as mobility devices (past and present), such as canes, crutches, wheelchairs, walkers; ability to climb stairs (like what floor is your laundry room or bedroom on); driving and/or sitting in a vehicle; weekend trips or vacations; personal hygiene and grooming; shopping; household chores (long list); cooking and doing dishes; laundry; social activities and relationships with spouse, family and friends; past and

Litigation Story

present hobbies; sporting activities; sexual activity or lack thereof (and frequently other embarrassing questions); sleeping patterns and how many times you awake with pain at night; yard/garden work, including mowing and snow removal; limitations in lifting, pushing, pulling bending, sitting, walking, standing—you name it!

I hate to use the word *always*, but what is *always* asked in a deposition:

Things you cannot do at all since the accident/injury, and things you can still do, but you experience pain or are limited in how well or for how long you can perform them.

A few of the pros of journaling to help encourage you are:

- organization and the great feeling it gives you
- preparedness
- enhances your creativity
- ability to keep track of important events, phone calls and communications, medical appointments and other appointments
- gives clarity of thought and memory improvement
- increases problem-solving capabilities
- aids in decision-making
- reduces stress and anxiety
- enables tracking of symptoms day to day, giving you the ability to recognize triggers and learn ways to better control them
- helps you make goals and progress toward your goals

I also feel that it is important to give you the heads-up on social media. In the past few years, social media's involvement in legal cases has increased rapidly. It is now common to see emails, Facebook posts, and text messages entered as evidence in depositions and at trials. Most of us have cell phones—cell phones with pictures that are preserved—and we use text messaging. Many people have an account with Facebook, Instagram, Twitter, Snapchat, WhatsApp, LinkedIn, and so on. You would be wise to not post anything regarding your accident, your injuries, or your health, including photographs.

Just as a simple example, a picture of you riding upside down in the Rock'n Roller Coaster at Disney would not support your testimony that your back pain keeps you from doing stuff! And what if the insurance

Stephanie Cousins

adjuster gets his hands on a snap of you shingling your roof the week you called in sick to work due to pain? And how about that Facebook post of you and your partner doin' the "Cotton-Eye Joe" at the nightclub when you've tried to convince others that you spend most of your days on the couch due to pain?

Such discoveries can have a massive impact on your case. A simple social media search could lead to discoverable evidence that might change everything for you. Be careful! Let me also add that you probably should not try to delete anything either. It scares me to say it, and it scares me that it's true, but it seems that everything can be recovered, even things we thought were buried long ago, and deleting information from social media could have the same consequences in a legal case as shredding physical documents.

Do not assume that privacy settings on your social media accounts mean anything. Instead, assume that anything posted on a public site for others to see can potentially be used in a lawsuit and that there is no reasonable expectation of privacy.

Your lawyer will advise you regarding doctors, work, insurance, medical bills, and so forth, and answer all your questions about your case. Keep a running list of questions you have for them for efficiency's sake. Time is money, especially if you are being billed. There is no such thing as a foolish question.

Write any questions or important information down in your journal, and underline or highlight them for your next appointment with your lawyer. Not only will this help to simplify your process along with your action; journaling also helps to process and download emotionally.

Remember, he or she is working *for you*, and not the other way around. He or she is deserving of your respect and appreciation as you work together. Do not be intimidated by the degree or the suit, or even the fancy office and big words, or fancy words and big office. They are just ordinary people, like you and me.

Caveat: Do not use Facebook or other social media to discuss your accident or injuries, and do not discuss your case with anyone other than your lawyer!

Litigation Story

Printouts of personal emails, text messages, and Facebook posts are often produced during a deposition, and you will likely be grilled about them.

You are not just another case, and your rights do matter. You will not allow *The System* to run you through the process like a cow headed to slaughter because you are quickly educating yourself about *how to be represented.* You will have all the knowledge, skills, and ability you need to move forward with great confidence that you are an intelligent and diligent litigant. A personal injury lawsuit or a worker's compensation claim does not have to ruin your life.

CHAPTER 10

Maintaining Peace while Moving Forward

If you can't sleep, then get up and do something instead of lying there worrying. It's the worry that gets you, not the lack of sleep.
—Dale Carnegie[1]

To maintain peace moving forward, at what may at times feel like a turtle's pace, bear in mind that your lawyer is responsible for dealing with many issues, filing necessary paperwork, investigation, interviewing, and deadlines, which require much time and energy. Determine that you will continue with your everyday life as much as possible, and do not dwell and meditate on your claim or lawsuit. Focusing on a lawsuit and/or misfortune will only make you miserable.

"How do I go on?" you may be asking. The answer is much simpler than you think. Here is the key: With *everything* that you do, do it as close to normal as you possibly can. In other words, get up at the same time of day you did before you were harmed or injured, *if* you are able, and carry on with your daily routine as close to normal as possible. Try not to deviate from your normal life any more than required, and do not impose unnecessary limitations or restrictions upon yourself. Do not let your habits and your routine reset any more than necessary, to help you cope and accommodate, because you do not want them to become your natural "default."

Litigation Story

Embrace the day and be thankful that you're not six feet under. Trauma is not a life sentence!

I'm not afraid to die, I just don't want to be there when it happens.
—Woody Allen[2]

My own personal journey of chronic neck pain, back pain, and headaches began at a very young age. In fact, it has been well more than two decades since I've experienced a totally pain-free day. I have spent many days of my life in bed, trying to ease the agony with rest, ice, heat, ointments, exercise, massage, chiropractic, physical therapy, over-the-counter medicines, behind-the-counter medicines, diet changes, meditation, naturopathy, electromagnetic stimulation (EMS), epidural injections, radiofrequency ablations, and surgery. The only thing I have not tried for pain is marijuana—yet.

I have missed countless activities with family and friends. I know times of being mad at myself, mad at God, and mad at the world because of my condition. I have continued to work over the last thirty-seven years in a job that requires continuous sitting with few breaks, intense concentration, spine-, head-, neck-, back-, shoulders-, arms-, and hands-torturing labor.

I know what it feels like to work in pain. It is possible. It is sometimes essential. Even early in my career, I began questioning my ability to continue in my field and whether or not I had the physical capability to be a court reporter. But at the same time, I was asking these questions: When did Americans decide that they deserve a pain-free life? When did I decide that I deserved a pain-free life? When did this great nation decide that we should not have to work with pain and that others should take care of us?

At the conclusion of my quest for answers, I came up with the grand finale question for myself: You're hurting anyway, right? Might as well be hurting at work, don't you think?

Am I eccentric? Maybe. But as it turns out, a massive amount of research indicates I am absolutely right. Ultimately, it is my belief that making myself live as close to normal as possible is what has kept me sane and alive, living a fabulous and adventurous life. But even beyond that, it

Stephanie Cousins

has emboldened me and given me a bulldog mentality that challenges me to do whatever it takes to accomplish what I set out to do.

> Character cannot be developed in ease and quiet. Only through experience of trial and suffering can the soul be strengthened, ambition inspired, and success achieved.
> —Helen Keller[3]

CHAPTER 11

To Work or Not to Work?

Sometimes pain can drive an individual harder than pleasure.

Chronic pain has been linked to numerous physical and mental conditions and contributes to high health care costs and lost productivity. In 2016, an estimated 20.4 percent of US adults had chronic pain and 8 percent of US adults had high-impact chronic pain.[1]

Thankfully, most people who testify that are injured have limitations that can be managed with care and attention, and they are still able to work and live a happy, productive life. Others have been faced with life-altering injuries and pain and have difficulty just making it through the day. They struggle with activities of daily living. They suffer from fatigue, struggle to make it to doctor's appointments, or even lose careers, hobbies, relationships, and so much more. Of course, there are those that are somewhere in-between.

It continually breaks my heart to listen to people testify who are living in horrible pain. In fact, some nights, I cannot even sleep because I'm thinking about how horrible that witness who testified that day must feel, and I try to imagine it myself. Having reported for so many years, I have become quite proficient at thinking about something else as I am writing, when necessary, when the testimony gets too sad, and I don't want to cry. But it does not always work.

And on the other hand, I must apply the same technique when the testimony is whiny, exaggerated, and delivered with fake and dramatic expressions of sheer agony! It is sometimes difficult to keep a straight face.

35

Stephanie Cousins

> Noise proves nothing. Often, a hen who has laid an
> egg crackles as if she had laid an asteroid.
> —Mark Twain[2]

For most of us who work, whether you believe it or not, your employer and/or coworkers have already sized you up; they've determined if you are a hard worker at your job or if you are the type of worker who avoids hard work as much as possible, doing just enough to get by.

> He that is good for making excuses is seldom good for anything else.
> —Benjamin Franklin[3]

In my career as a court reporter working with significant pain, it has always bothered me to observe people who refuse to work because they hurt. Just where did our society get the idea that you do not have to work when you hurt? Our great nation was built by men and women who worked despite great pain, disease, old age, malnutrition, famine, freezing temperatures, extremely hot temperatures, scurvy, dysentery, age-related illnesses, and every medical condition known to humankind.

For more than twenty years, I have traveled to different parts of the world participating in disaster relief efforts, and I've personally observed how other cultures deal with pain, trauma, and life-altering events that threatened to destroy them and destroy their lives. It has been fascinating, to say the least. Each particular people group has its own language of pain and distress, and each has its own unique way of expressing pain and suffering, depending on such things as whether their religion and culture values or does not value the display of emotions and verbal expressions of pain or injury. Some cultural groups expect an extravagant display of emotion in the presence of pain. Other cultures value stoicism (the quality or behavior of a person who accepts what happens without complaining or showing emotion), restraint, and downplaying of pain.

I have spent a great deal of time in Africa, and if you ask someone how they "feel," the question does not even make sense to them. For them, it is a confusing and irrelevant question. They are not a me-focused people group, for the most part. I have discovered that Southeast Asians tend to advocate that people should keep their pain to themselves. In rural Nepal,

36

Litigation Story

it appears that the symptoms of back pain are not perceived to be a medical issue but rather part of the aging processes. Of course, in some cultures, women cannot be *fully* examined by a male doctor, and there are no female doctors, so they suffer in silence.

We are all probably familiar with the statement my father would make, "Don't cry, or I'll give you something to cry about." As I am sure you know, many cultures instill in their children, beginning at a very young age, to behave bravely and not cry, particularly boys.

I have witnessed in Asia men and women after burial rituals lying on graves, crying and wailing for a few days as they mourned, and then suddenly ceasing, believing that grieving for the deceased will heap greater punishment upon the decedent as they enter eternity. I remember being so saddened by this information when I considered the guilt and fear this would cause a new widow and her children.

Have you ever studied the human tragedy of the Holocaust and the working conditions of the concentration labor camps—the suffering and torment? They continued working because they had to. It was work or die. Physical harassment of the prisoners resulted in numerous broken limbs and sores that would never heal, usually after flogging; sexual barbarity; pneumonia; frostbite that would develop into gangrene; dreadful sanitation conditions causing dysentery, skin diseases, and scabies; boils, rashes, and abscesses that resulted from vitamin deficiency and infections; typhus; starvation; aborted pregnancies; tuberculosis; impaired vision and hearing; memory loss; nervous breakdowns; and exhaustion to the point of collapse. Most prisoners suffered from several medical conditions simultaneously.

How did they do it? How did they continue to work? These are atrocities that the human mind cannot comprehend. It is impossible for us to understand how they did it, but we can learn much about their drive and perseverance.

When we are no longer able to change a situation,
we are challenged to change ourselves.
Forces beyond your control can take away everything you possess except one thing, your freedom to choose how you will respond to the situation.
Our greatest freedom is the freedom to choose our attitude.
—Holocaust survivor Viktor Frank[4]

Stephanie Cousins

We kept speculating what would happen, because when you are alive, you don't give up hope. I was hopeful that something would happen."
—Holocaust survivor Martin Weiss[5]

I don't want to have lived in vain like most people. I want to be useful or bring enjoyment to all people, even those I've never met. I want to go on living even after my death!"
—Anne Frank[6]

But miracles still happen, even if we don't think they do."
—Holocaust survivor Diet Eman[7]

May these words give you hope, determination, strength, and courage in the face of the adversity you are encountering. We all come from a long line of overcomers. Never give up hope!

Can you do an experiment and continue a workday, or a partial workday, even if you hurt? *If* you can work through pain, or despite pain—Try it!—if your doctor has cleared you. Let me stress that you should follow your doctor's advice, unless it goes against your conscience (conscience means with knowledge). Working will give you a sense of value, purpose, and connection, among other things, and will also help to keep your mind off your own personal situation and pain, with dignity intact.

I know it gets harder when we age. Oh, boy, do I know. But do not be self-restricted by age. Mark Twain said that age is an issue of mind over matter. If you don't mind, it doesn't matter.[8]

You must make your own choice about whether to work or not. For me personally, to decline work when one can work seems illogical, despite what it may look like to a trier of fact, but you do what you are convinced that you should do. You are the one that matters.

If you *are* still able to work and have chosen to work, go to work and do the absolute best job you can. Give it all you've got and work as if it was your first day on the job. Do not baby any body parts that you don't have to. Don't wince or distort your face every time you move. And don't exaggerate a limp or pain. We call those people "malingerers," and they are easily identified by coworkers and jurors. Don't do it!

Litigation Story

Merriam-Webster's definition of malingering is "to pretend or exaggerate incapacity or illness (as to avoid duty or work)."

Wikipedia's definition of malingering is "the fabricating of symptoms of mental or physical disorders for a variety of 'secondary gain' motives, which may include financial compensation (often tied to fraud), avoiding school, work, or military service, obtaining drugs, getting lighter criminal sentences, or simply to attract attention or sympathy."

The Diagnostic and Statistical Manual of Mental Disorders, Fifth Edition (DSM-5) describes malingering as "the intentional production of false or grossly exaggerated physical or psychological problems."

True, you may be *in pain* or *have pain* in some parts of your body, but chances are that more than half of the people you are surrounded by hurt somewhere too. We all have a story, and some people have told their story so many times that it truly becomes "their story." It becomes a part of their identity that they have foolishly come to accept. But it does not have to become your new identity or your destiny. I know it is challenging, but don't feel sorry for yourself. It's just a part of life.

The following chronic pain statistics are taken from the American Academy of Pain Medicine, National Institutes of Health, American Chiropractic Association, and American Society of Addiction Medicine:

Chronic Pain Statistics in the United States[9]

- Pain affects more people in the United States than diabetes, heart disease, and cancer combined.
- 126 million, or 55 percent of all adults, experienced pain in the previous three months.
- 4 million US adults report "a lot of pain."
- 3 million US adults suffer from daily pain.
- Various reports list that over fifty million, but up to one hundred million, US adults have chronic pain conditions, an estimate that does not include acute pain conditions or children in pain.
- More than one-quarter of adults (26 percent) age twenty years and over—or an estimated 76.5 million people—report that they have

Stephanie Cousins

had a problem with pain of any sort that persisted for more than twenty-four hours.

- Of those in pain, 27 percent suffer from lower back pain, 15 percent from severe headache or migraine pain, and 15 percent from neck pain.

It seems to be a common theme during depositions that people will testify, after being read entries in their medical records, that there are errors, sometimes egregious errors. For example, the nature of injury or how their injury occurred, past medical history, comments made during an examination, dates, recommendations upon discharge from the emergency room, and even diagnoses. It is important to know what's in your own medical records, if you can get your hands on them.

You may only be permitted to work part time because of your injury or pain, and some people may not be able to work at all. A lot of people do not know they were put on maximum medical improvement (MMI), or even what MMI is. A good definition of maximum medical improvement is the point at which the condition of an injured person is stabilized, and no further recovery or improvement is expected even with additional medical intervention. Basically, a condition is at maximum medical improvement if it is not believed that the condition will change or progress.[10]

Some people are not informed that they can request vocational assistance from their employer/work comp. Vocational rehabilitation is made up of a series of services that are designed to facilitate the entrance into or return to work by people with disabilities or by people who have recently acquired an injury or disability. Some of these services include vocational assessment and evaluation, training, upgrading of general skills, refresher courses, on-the-job training, career counseling, employment searches, and consulting with potential or existing employers for job accommodations and modification. These services may also vary depending on the needs of the individual.[11]

Others never realized their restrictions had been lifted or changed, and you would not believe the number of people who never knew they had been released to return to work. Who do we blame for this lack of communication and lack of information sharing?

If you can work, then try to work—*if your doctors have cleared you to*

Litigation Story

work! If you are hurting, what is the difference if you're hurting at work or if you're hurting at home? Does it truly matter *where* you are hurting? At least if you are working, and not sitting at home, you're not focusing on *yourself.* Focusing on oneself is enough to make anybody miserable, and it only intensifies pain.

And again, do not be a complainer. A lot of people will never get to where they want to be because they will not stop complaining. I am not saying you don't have anything to complain about. I am just saying it won't do you any good.

This requires repeating: Don't complain—any more than necessary. Nobody likes to be around that!

> Be grateful for what you have, and stop complaining—it bores everybody else, does you no good, and doesn't solve any problems.
> —Zig Ziglar[12]

You give strength to what you focus on the most. Check it out for yourself. Focus for a few minutes on where you feel some pain right now, and see if it does not escalate. This is called the law of attraction.

Be the victor in your battle with pain and be aggressive with your recovery. What do I mean by that? You do not have to *feel* like exercising or going to physical therapy in order to do it. Put on those loose-fitting clothes, and get to it! You are only one decision away from rehabilitating your body.

Make sure you keep all your doctor's appointments, and be truthful and complete with him or her. Don't try to hide anything, and don't exaggerate anything either. Follow your doctor's advice, if you trust your doctor, regarding work, exercise, medication, and everything he or she has to offer.

Do your absolute best if you are undergoing physical therapy and follow your doctor's and therapist's advice closely. Do not cut corners. The problem is that rehabilitation can hurt; it is tiring, and it gets old fast. But please understand this: If you do not do what you're supposed to do, you will probably have a slow or incomplete recovery. You don't want that, do you?

Work hard at your rehabilitation, and consider it a job. You will probably have to push through pain. Yes, it hurts! I guarantee that most of

Stephanie Cousins

the people you see at rehab working hard hurt, too, and they also kept their appointment regardless of how they *felt*. Do not miss those appointments unless it is absolutely necessary. Do not talk yourself out of it!

It cannot be emphasized enough that you cannot improve physically, with mobility, if you refuse to do what is prescribed for you—*exercise*! Goals are going to be set, and goals can be fun. Set your mind ahead of time! Fight for what you want. Your attitude is absolutely everything, and your personal positive outlook can speed up the healing process and lessen the emotional pain you are going through.

A body in motion, stays in motion; a body at rest, stays at rest.
—Sir Isaac Newton[13]

This is an absolute truth. You can *never* recover from an injury without exercise. Yes, it may hurt, but you're hurting anyway; right? Pushing through pain may possibly be your key, again, if your doctor prescribes it, and you are physically able.

Rest assured, there will be ups and downs during your recovery, but do not get disheartened. This is just a part of the recovery process and is perfectly normal. I think one of the most difficult aspects of an accident or injury is that you can't do what you normally do, and over your lifetime, these activities have been a continual source of self-esteem, satisfaction, meaning, and joy in life. But please remember, and remind yourself daily, this is only a season of my life; it won't last forever, and I'm going to make it through as a champion. People are gonna be amazed!

Don't listen to that voice that says, "You might as well give up. You're not getting anywhere anyway. It's doing more harm than good." This self-sabotaging talk only sets you up for failure. Silence the negative voices, whether they are within or without. Take courage and conquer your fears head-on. I would suggest to you that having courage means you are afraid, but you're still moving. Replace that lie with: "I'm taking things one day at a time, and I'm going to keep walking, moving, living, and persevering." Perseverance means *to bear up under pressure*. You can do it! You are going to have an amazing recovery and rebound with a victory.

CHAPTER 12

The Waiting Game

Whatever course you decide upon, there is always someone to
tell you that you are wrong. There are always difficulties arising
which tempt you to believe that your critics are right. To map out
a course of action and follow it to an end requires courage.
—Ralph Waldo Emerson[1]

If you are still reading, you have probably already secured a lawyer and
supplied him or her with the required information necessary to get the
ball rolling. Take a deep breath. Everything is going to be fine. Take
some time to regroup, and be confident that you have made the right
decision.

Returning to your normal routine as much as possible is a particularly
important component to acceptance and recovery after an injury/accident.
But having said that, I would also encourage you to give yourself the time
you need and be patient with what you are pushing through. We are all
different, and you do not have to prove any*thing* to any*body*!

Taking care of yourself both physically and emotionally at this stage
is vitally important. It is also one of the most difficult things to do at this
tender time because your life has been thrown into upheaval, and you hurt.
But you can do it!

Whether you think you can, or you think you can't—you're right.
—Henry Ford[2]

Stephanie Cousins

Make plans for your day, even in the simple and mundane things. Try to stick to your preaccident/preinjury routine as much as possible and create new awesome habits as well. You must live, move, and breathe whether you *feel* like it or not, but you're hurting either way, right? Do that very thing that you don't *feel* like doing. You have greater power than *how you feel*. Again, I cannot stress it enough, do that very *thing* you don't want to do, like getting out of bed, bathing, cooking, cleaning, exercising, expressing your sexuality, studying, listening to uplifting music, going outdoors when possible, and engaging in social activities. It's not falling that's the worst; it's staying on the ground.

A popular ancient saying is: "This too shall pass." That does not mean the suffering from all trials and tribulations always goes away. The emotional and physical scarring from some experiences can truly be deep and can leave us with long-term weak spots and vulnerabilities. But in most cases, we are tougher than we think, and we have some say in how long we remain injured, and to what degree. If you have put yourself in neutral, this is a fantastic opportunity for greater faith.

It does take great faith to say, "This too shall pass," but say it anyway. This season of your life will not last forever, and you are off to a great start. The mere fact that you are reading this book and trying to map out your best path proves that you are in control and living intentionally. You are *not* going to be totally occupied with yourself and what happened to you.

Humility is not thinking less of yourself; it's thinking of yourself less.
—C. S. Lewis[3]

Oh, how many hundreds of people I have sat with who are occupied, almost exclusively, with themselves. Do not let it be you! Make the decision right now that you will not give in to this life destroyer. Refuse to constantly be occupied with focusing on yourself and the condition of your body, but instead learn the art of refocusing your thoughts on positive things in your life. Great thinking precedes great achievement.

Please seek counseling if you need it. If you are depressed or have constant irritability, significantly reduced interest or feeling no pleasure in activities, significant weight loss or weight gain, a decrease or increase in appetite, insomnia or an increased desire to sleep, tiredness or loss of

Litigation Story

energy, these symptoms may mean that you are in need of some qualified outside support. Seeking the help of a professional therapist or counselor is not a sign of weakness. On the contrary, it is a sign of strength.

If you are having suicidal thoughts, seek professional help immediately. You can get support from the National Suicide Prevention Hotline at 1-800-273-8255.

There are literally dozens of avenues for those who cannot afford to pay for a professional, and there are teachings by the hundreds just for your particular problem area. The library is free, and they have books, tapes, DVDs, videos, and all kinds of helps. Get your hands on some! The internet is jam-packed and overflowing with help tailored just for you.

You will be a serious student of an overcoming life if you would just begin to act, and continue, and continue, and continue. Read, read, read everything that you can lay your hands on about how to improve your life situation. There is no excuse these days for lack of knowledge, for those who desire to learn. Train yourself, and become a master in positive living. I promise you that your friends and family will see an amazing change in you that money cannot buy!

I am quite sure we all have people in our lives that we try to spend as little time with as possible because all they do is complain or try to extract sympathy out of you; and I'm also certain that we've all known people that have been injured or are in severe pain (disabilities and chronic illnesses) and you would never know it by their words or actions.

The first group of gripers are very me-focused (and boring, by the way); and the second group of individuals (the ones that are pleasant to be around), are the standard of a free and wonderful life, despite pain, who are enjoying their life to the fullest. Not only that, but they are constantly trying to help others who deal with pain because they can so readily relate to their suffering.

What kind of person are you? Do you need to change? Can you change? Do you want to change?

> It is not death that a man should fear, but he
> should fear never beginning to live.
> —Marcus Aurelius[4]

Stephanie Cousins

It is your choice to give up or to endure and keep walking. Of course, there are days where you want to give up, and you are feeling so defeated and disheartened. That's OK, and that's normal. Do not beat yourself up over it. Go to bed early and get some rest, knowing that you did the best you could today. Tomorrow is a new day.

When that new day comes, get out of bed on purpose, with a smile on your face, brush the dirt of the world off, and soldier on! I promise you, the more you practice being grateful for a new day, the easier it is going to be the next time you have a bad day. You will be able to face it head-on because you have been practicing intentional living.

Simple and practical advice:

1. Get out of bed whether you want to or not.
2. Make plans for your day, no matter how big or small.
3. Eat when you don't feel like eating, unless you need to lose weight.
4. Walk even if it hurts, if you are able.
5. Stretch that body and get some form of exercise. Remove any potential obstacles ahead of time. Have your exercise attire and gear ready, juice or water in hand, and get to it.
6. Smile even if you don't feel like it.
7. Learn how to laugh at yourself.
8. As a part of your journaling, write down at least one good thing that happened today, and refer to it when you need encouragement.
9. Surround yourself with things that encourage you—photographs, sayings, scripture, jokes. Post sticky notes on your mirrors, on your refrigerator, and in your car.
10. Care about how you look each day. Fix yourself up like company was coming over. Sounds vain, but this can be a tremendous boost, especially for those who must look at you. I always say, "I wear makeup for your protection!"
11. Do not keep your "helps" out in the open for you and everybody else to look at: ice packs, heating pads, medicine, Biofreeze (super great), Tylenol. These are just reminders to you and to everyone else.

Litigation Story

An accident or injury does not have to destroy your life, and trauma is not a life sentence. There are simple, everyday choices you are going to have to make, and these are choices that you make upstairs—in your head. Start applying the principles in this book and begin to implement these simple and effective tools. Hold your head up high. You are one of a kind, and there is no one like you.

CHAPTER 13

Testifying

When you go into court, you are putting yourself in the hands of twelve people that weren't smart enough to get out of jury duty.
—Norm Crosby

On average, people rate their fear of public speaking higher than their fear of death. Unfortunately, according to Merrie Jo Pitera, PhD, chief executive officer of Litigation Insights and a psychology and communications expert who specializes in complex litigation and trial consulting, with twenty-nine years of experience in the field, anxiety is the number one communication obstacle in legal proceedings.[1]

I have discovered over my years as a court reporter that some people genuinely care about how they come across to people, and others couldn't care less. But if you are going to testify, prepare yourself. You would be foolish not to. Don't get me wrong. I'm not saying you want to be an actor at all, as happiness comes when we are in a place of being our true, authentic selves and making choices that are in line with who we are as an individual. But we should always care about how we present ourselves to others. A proverb says, "Being respected is more important than having great riches. To be well thought of is better than owning silver or gold."

I remember particular witnesses, and whether I believed that they were genuinely interested in their own recovery and overall healing or whether I didn't believe them, or whether I didn't feel the least bit sorry for them, and whether I believed that they were their own worst enemy against recovery.

I think it is necessary that I list a few common examples of witness behavior that worked against the person, from my personal view only, and

Litigation Story

then let you judge for yourself. I believe that these behaviors and attitudes were so obvious and egregious, in my opinion, that anyone could spot it, including a judge or jury, and you would not believe how common these types of scenarios are. It may sound harsh and nonsympathetic, but how they "came across" made me want to say these things to them:

"Did you not think the other lawyer was going to ask you if you always use that cane or if you just used it today for the deposition?"

"If the doctor prescribed walking as your best solution to your ailment, can't you keep doing it even when it hurts? You're hurting anyway; right? You cannot improve your mobility because you refuse to do what the doctor prescribed—*exercise*."

"I'm sorry that you were asked, 'Have you gained weight since your injury?' But you are going to continue to gain weight and be out of shape unless you get some form of daily exercise *and* you burn more calories than you consume. I know it hurts! But if you are less active now due to your accident/injury, your eating is going to have to change for a while, too, if you do not want to gain weight."

"Some people want somebody else to pay for their lack of discipline. Is that person you?"

"Thank you for clarifying that your basketball exploits, your running, waterskiing, bowling, and weight-lifting days were in high school. I thought you were talking about the time right before your accident!"

"You may think that dosing and overdosing on alcohol and narcotics is easing your pain, but it is also causing a lot of your pain and problems: constipation, fatigue, sadness, stomach issues, restlessness, and possibly dependency. Does the relief you are getting outweigh the negative consequences?"

"You sound kind of bitter and mean, and you're saying that you've lost friends because you don't feel good, and you can't go out anymore. Are you sure that's the reason?"

"You're bored, and you think it's everyone else's fault. You need to take responsibility for your time and activities. We are all given twenty-four hours in a day. Why do you throw them away!"

Either run the day or the day runs you.
—Jim Rohn[2]

Stephanie Cousins

"You are doing everything you can to make people feel sorry for you, to get stuff: free rides, money, attention, free labor. Stop it!"

"If you say you do not want to be a burden to others, then, don't be—if at all possible. Why don't you do what you can to help yourself *and* others, and push through that pain when you can. You can do more than you realize, and it will expedite your recovery. Remember, your condition is tough on everybody."

"Did you know that helping someone else will help take your mind off your condition, your pain, yourself? Serve somebody else, whether big or small, and you will both be blessed."

You do not have to *feel* like helping someone else in order to help somebody else. You do not have to *feel* like exercising in order to get up and do some exercise. You do not have to *feel* like grabbing some groceries in order to go do it. You will never accomplish anything if you never do stuff despite how you *"feel."* Live in the moment. My father always used to say, "If you're not where you're at, you're nowhere." When I now look back on it in my older years, wow, was he wise.

"Oh, come on! Do you really want to blame *that*, too, on your injury? You can still be a source of help and encouragement to your family, friends, and coworkers, even when you are suffering yourself. Not only is it possible, but it will return great joy to you. Quit ignoring the rest of your household and family!"

"Do you honestly want people to believe that you and your partner used to engage in intimate activity fifteen times a week before your injury?"

"And how is life working out for you in the recliner? Is it really someone else's fault, or were you like this before? Do you believe it's possible to live a good life from the recliner?"

Have I ever encountered a witness living a good life from the recliner? I have never seen anyone do it who has not become lazy, mean, pointing fingers, and blaming everybody else for their problems.

"You've bought into the lie that it's better to collect money for disability than to work at an actual job. If your doctor has cleared you to work, full time, part time, light duty or full duty, give it all you've got—*unless you don't got it."*

"If you are unable to return to your old job, for physical reasons or other reasons, seek some other form of employment if you can. It may not

Litigation Story

be your dream job, but it may turn out to be the best job you ever had. Ask your lawyer about procuring vocational rehabilitation services. Stay in the game of life, and be a part of society. You are valuable, and the world needs you. Your confidence and self-esteem will continue to improve."

"Didn't you know that the lawyer questioning you was going to have access to *all* your prior health history and medical records?"

I understand that just making it through an ordinary day sometimes seems like climbing a mountain. I've climbed many of those mountains myself. But I've seen it become a trap for many individuals who were once strong and confident, who begin to feel unproductive and inadequate because of their condition. You are greater than how you *feel*, and you've got so much to accomplish in this life!

"Oh, my goodness, you need to pay attention to your physical appearance, for your own sake. Get out of those sweatpants and slippers (yes, I've seen witnesses show up wearing slippers), bathe, put on some wonderful cologne or perfume, for no reason at all, and see if you feel better about yourself."

> "Do yourself a favor and quit saying:
> To be honest …
> To be totally honest …
> To tell you the truth …
> In all honesty …
> Truthfully …
> Honestly …
> It makes it sound like you are not truthful and honest all
> the time. Are you being truthful and honest?"

When in doubt, look intelligent.
—Garrison Keillor[3]

"You're married, and you haven't had relations with your partner for how long? Surely there is some way to "work this out," for mercy's sake! Remember your marriage vows if you believe in them. So what if the physical act stresses your back, neck, hip, whatever. Sex has been divinely created to feel good and take a relationship to heights that are impossible

Stephanie Cousins

to attain through any other means, and it can be a great tension reliever. Remember?"

"Are you truthfully trying to tell us that you now smoke for stress solely because of your injuries? How many packs a day did you smoke prior to your accident?" (Believe me, you will be asked!)

"Can you do your best to pull yourself out of bed in the morning to watch a sunrise, or drag yourself away from the TV long enough to watch a sunset? Get away from that TV!"

"If we seek out the testimony of your children, under oath, will they testify that you used to be a great parent until 'all this happened'? Will records disclose that your children only 'began' to manifest bad behavior after your injury? Will your spouse say you were the best spouse in the world prior to your accident?"

"OK. You were limping on the other leg before we took a break. What's up with that?"

Of course, I never said any of this to any witness. As a court reporter, we do not engage in any conversation with a witness outside of niceties and general short conversation. I have never seen a time when there have been so many bitter, angry, and touchy people in the world. From my personal observation, a lot of people want somebody else to pay for their lack of discipline, self-control, and lack of decent behavior. It is not pleasant to be around, and outside of work, I try to avoid people like that at all costs. They will drain the life right out of you.

Do not try to draw attention to yourself with exaggerated facial expressions or verbal expressions of pain. It is ugly, and everybody picks up on it. Do not overexaggerate a limp or try to draw attention to a body part that you are gripping in agony. And don't lie!

I know it sounds judgmental, but to my perception, scores and scores of people testifying who have had an accident or injury try to convince the "triers of fact" and family and friends that every bad thing in their life was a result of what's happened to them. It doesn't work.

You can be fully prepared and confident to answer tough questions (and there will be tough questions), void of all fear and intimidation. Again, prepare yourself!

CHAPTER 14

Don't Let the System Drag You Down

It has grieved me to watch how some lawyers seem to further enable their client to remain stuck where they are in order to enhance their suit, instead of giving them solid advice that they personally and professionally know would help. This approach keeps their clients bound in chains and dependent on them, which is cruel, arrogant, and does not help an injured individual move toward healing and wholeness. I would have to say that in all my thirty-seven years of firsthand observation, this particular subject is what I have been most passionate about as I have listened to people testify.

For instance, many people testify during their deposition that they were never told that they have been medically released by their physicians to return to work when, in fact, they were released. They will say neither their attorney nor their physician had told them. People are often unaware that the medical restrictions they had received immediately after their accident/injury have been increased, decreased, or entirely lifted. Scores of people who testify cannot ever tell you what their weight-lifting restrictions are, if their restrictions include bending, lifting, pushing, pulling, standing, sitting, walking, and on and on and on. This bears repeating; countless individuals testify they do not know if and when they reached maximum medical improvement—MMI. People will say that they were never given the option of receiving vocational rehabilitation counseling.

Are they all forgetful, lying, or is it a lack of communication?

Yes, there are fabulous lawyers out there, and I have worked with hundreds of them. The lawyers that I have considered top-notch do not participate in what I'm describing; but it has really troubled me over the

Stephanie Cousins

years to see how some attorneys often enable their clients to perpetuate their *victim mentality*. I don't know that they do this on purpose necessarily, although, I'm quite certain many do, but their bad advice and lack of advice, and ongoing negative instructions, suggestions, and innuendoes all scream, "You have to convince the jury or judge how bad you are!" It seems to be all about what you can convince the trier of fact.

> Client: I'll give you $500 to do my worrying for me.
> Lawyer: Fine. Where's the $500?
> Client: That will be your first worry.

By the same token, many injured people place restrictions on themselves, even when their doctors have not prescribed restrictions, because "it hurts," or they are more concerned with convincing doctors, lawyers, and judges that working is impossible for them and that they are just helpless victims. Some people are so focused on making their condition appear so bad that they end up severely hindering their own recovery.

And while it is true that lots of people are trying their best to heal and achieve a great recovery, they are afraid of not accurately portraying how they are really doing. They want to get their point across with no apologies. The problem is that people will adopt this approach to their life, and it becomes a part of their personality. Maybe unintentional, but at the same time, doing much more damage to their lives and their ability to cope, adjust, find new and creative ways of doing things, making adaptations necessary and helpful—again, paralyzing them. So, what starts out to be just a simple approach to litigation or a workers' compensation claim turns into a watered-down, powerless, unhappy version of who you really are and what your potential is.

I understand that lawyers have a lot of clients and that letters, medical information, insurance approvals, and so on, often move extremely slow, which sometimes attorneys have less control over, but ridiculous is ridiculous! If a person did not start out with depression and anxiety after an accident or injury, the time-altering process can certainly bring it on, exacerbate it, or bring someone to his or her knees in hopelessness.

For me, the workers' compensation process has always blown my mind, and it seems to be much like an automated conveyor-belt process.

Litigation Story

What rights does the injured have when being slowly driven through this complicated system of doctors, exams, treatment, evaluations, rehabilitation, therapies, and disability? Shouldn't the injured have a voice too? Make sure your lawyer allows you to be a part of the decision-making process, especially if you are being made to feel like offers and decisions are over your head.

It is important for me to mention that you may be asked to submit to an IME, which is an independent medical examination, which really isn't independent at all. The insurance company will *pay* a doctor to examine you and give an opinion about your injury, the cause of your injury, your ability to work, future medical treatment you may require, and disability. Does that sound "independent" to you?

If you are involved in a work injury, quite often, your employer's insurance company will ask for an IME if they disagree with your own doctor's diagnosis, especially if it involves extensive medical treatment, surgery, or permanent disability (thousands of dollars). Attorneys and insurance companies are very careful in selecting a doctor who historically will say the patient is fine and ready to go back to work, having only reviewed a few records and spent only a few minutes talking with the patient, never even laying a hand on the patient—and then out the door you go.

People most typically testify that they were rushed in and rushed out the door, never having been asked relevant questions to form an honest and fair opinion. Furthermore, the physician performing the so-called *independent* medical examination will never speak to the patient regarding the examination or evaluation results—I mean after all, you're just an IME report to him or her, which can mean thousands and thousands of dollars a year for that doctor, apart from the doctor's *treating practice*. Not a bad gig, aye?

I personally would never attend an independent medical examination without first talking to an experienced lawyer. Bear in mind, because it is an "independent" exam by a doctor, that you have no doctor-patient relationship with the doctor, and you should expect no confidentiality. Anything you say to him or her can become a part of the report, so watch what you say.

Stephanie Cousins

> *Warning*: Sometimes, the insurance company will look at your social media accounts to see if what you are chatting about and posting is different than what you report to your employer or your doctors.

> *Warning*: It's important to understand that you could be under surveillance at any time by the insurance company and under the scrutiny of a camera. There is really no privacy anymore.

We do have what I believe is the best legal system and medical system in the world. But come on!

One of the most common witness complaints is addressing his or her treating physicians, being bounced around from doctor to doctor, and doctors rushing the person in and out, with little to no recommendations or information. I'm quite certain that we have all experienced that.

While I was waiting for a rhizotomy, also known as a nerve ablation, I waited more than six weeks to get in to see my doctor, and I was in the middle of the worst pain storm of my life. After my long-awaited medical appointment, I was told that they had to wait for my insurance company, Blue Cross/Blue Shield, to approve the procedure. I waited another three weeks, until in desperation I called my insurance company to ask what the hold-up was. When they told me that the procedure did not need their approval (because of my prior medical history and earlier procedures and attempts at pain relief), and that my doctor's office had been informed more than a week prior, I was livid.

I had been continuing the best I could, managing my pain the best way I knew how, and trying my hardest to stay positive. My patience was running short, I admit. I generally try to be understanding of how busy medical offices are. In some states, it takes much longer to get in for a procedure—and especially long for those who are suffering from severe pain, the elderly, and our veterans.

Come on! Can you at least pretend that I matter?

Run your case. Don't let your case run you. Carrying on with life and work during these extremely difficult times is challenging but essential. Not to say I didn't complain and whine to my spouse, feel sorry for myself

Litigation Story

and, admittedly, use my *pain card* a few times over the years. But I have kept living, and living a wonderful life, despite these seasons of ups and downs. The only other option is to become bitter and angry, which only increases pain and anxiety, and, thus, the cycle goes on.

Chronic pain is awful, but it does not have to destroy your life. I truly understand how easily it can, and I also understand through experience that we do not have to allow it. Take whatever drastic measures you must take to continue not only coping but thriving. My dictionary defines *thrive* this way: To progress toward or realize a goal despite or because of circumstances. Lots of individuals in the middle of a health storm will not take any medicine, prescribed or over the counter, because of other medical complications, because they don't like how it makes them feel, or they just don't believe in taking medicine. With all the current medical hype about narcotic addiction, who could blame them? I really don't know how they do it, though!

I have heard witnesses speak of waiting weeks for approval for a cane, a walker, other essential medical devices that they will often pay for themselves, praying that the insurance company will reimburse them eventually. Good luck with those forms! I remember a particular witness claiming to have waited three weeks after a foot break in an accident for the insurance company to approve surgery, and that foot had already reset and reset poorly.

Do not be afraid to contact your lawyer, your doctor, or your employer when you need to. They are getting paid to do what they do. Just have your questions and requests prepared, succinct and to the point, and find out whatever you can about what your options are. Be polite, but do not let anyone intimidate you. You have rights, your rights matter, and you matter. Hold your head up and keep walking. You are valuable and deserve humane treatment. No, I am not saying come in hot, acting like a bully. If you want respect, you must be respectable. Nobody, including you, likes to be screamed at and disrespected; and it gets you nowhere.

After having exhausted all other options, with ever-increasing pain, numbness, and tingling in my head, neck, shoulder, arm, hand, and fingers, I was approved for a cervical disc replacement, an actual titanium disc. I was excited, which is weird, I know. But if you have these kinds of symptoms, you know exactly what I'm speaking of.

Stephanie Cousins

Then *the plague* struck—yes, COVID-19! All elective procedures were off the table for what seemed like forever. I implemented the recommendations and instructions in this book regarding intentional living—stretching and exercise, healthy eating, plenty of rest and relaxation, policing my focus and what I'm thinking and saying, personal strategies for pain relief—and surrounded myself with a positive environment to the extent I was able, which included allowing counseling and encouragement from friends and family. I did the best I knew how and continued working as a court reporter to the fullest extent possible. What else could I do?

I had days where I felt like I was barely getting by, and I had days where I felt like I was soaring like an eagle, despite my painful predicament. Conversely, I had some days where I felt like the biggest loser in the world, stuck in self-pity and trying to convince myself that I had no business writing this book. What a hypocrite, I thought! This is normal for people living with chronic pain, but it is excessive and harmful if those thoughts last longer than minutes and hours.

I am happy to say that I finally was able to have the surgery done and am wonderfully recovering. Please understand, I know I am so far from having *anything* perfected as a person and will never apply all I've learned perfectly; but I am learning more each day, through trial and error and many painful mistakes. But I believe so passionately about what I have learned from my own suffering and from watching and listening to other stories of suffering over the course of my career that I want to help as many people as I can come through their trauma and suffering with a victory, even if pain remains, like some of mine has. Is it easy? Of course not. But what in life is easy?

Theodore Roosevelt said that nothing worth having comes easy. For the history buffs, you know that Theodore Roosevelt was our twenty-sixth US president. But did you know that he had asthma, was blind in one eye, was once shot in the chest, and, in 1884, lost his first wife and mother on the same day? Perhaps this great man knew what he was talking about.

I remember many days over the years of beating myself up with shame because I just needed to stay in bed for a day and *collect myself.* As it turns out, this is very therapeutic for me, physically and mentally, and after allowing myself a day in bed, I am fired up and ready to go the next day. I have also allowed myself a weekend to do the same, reassessing my life and

58

Litigation Story

my goals. Goals are extremely important no matter who you are. Without them, we have no direction and no way to gauge where we are. If you do not have goals for yourself, how do you measure your capability? What do you have to reach for, or how do you know when you're oh so close? How will you know when you have arrived? We constantly and consistently need a goal in front of us to encourage us as we live this life.

Make it your purpose to pursue a lifelong journey of goals that never end until you are on the other side of eternity. Set them high! Also, bear in mind that the reason we set goals and make plans is so we can have goals and plans to modify along the way, as necessary and appropriate, while keeping the overall purpose alive. Those who endure to the end succeed. If I had not set goals for myself, I never would have made it this far. I know that I have not arrived yet, but I'm still living, moving, and pressing on one day at a time.

> I've failed over and over and over again in
> my life, and that is why I succeed.
> —Michael Jordan[1]

Many times I have missed important events because of real pain, and I've been good to myself all day and did not allow it to beat me up and condemn me. I have also had days where I've done nothing but beat myself up all day. Have you done this?

"You're an uncaring dad or mom. Why couldn't you just go to that ball game and watch your poor child?"

"Well, because the thought of sitting on bleachers makes me want to gouge my eyes out."

Or perhaps you hear, "So what? Do it anyway, for the kid. Otherwise, they may think you don't love them or care about their activities."

What a crock! If you are doing your job as a parent, your children are going to know you love them regardless of your attendance at their events. Sadly, there are always parents who try to guilt you into participating in events and activities, which typically boils down to time and money. After all, the little darlings might wind up with rejection issues. It's all a big lie! Could this be why we have a generation that is so into themselves

Stephanie Cousins

and how wonderful they are that statistics show they take more pictures of themselves than anyone else?

It is necessary that you do what you can to live, work, and breathe through your pain and problems, but don't be so harsh with yourself that you live a life of shame and guilt. Do not worry about what other people think all the time. They do not know what you have been through, and they don't walk in your shoes.

"I finally stopped caring what other people think!

I hope everyone is OK with that?"

You are, no doubt, going to have high days and low days. This does not mean you are bipolar. It means you are human, and we live in a world that at times feels like a roller coaster. Apart from my own faith, I doubt it is even possible for me to live a meaningful and wonderful life on this roller coaster. I probably would have thrown in the towel a long time ago. I'm just being honest. But I am here to tell you that it is possible.

Furthermore, if you set out to apply at least some of the principles in this book, you will take a dramatic upswing. Life is going to go on with or without your participation. Wouldn't you rather play this reality game? Adventure into the unknown and experience a life spent challenging yourself, investigating yourself, and proving truths and dispelling lies regarding what you believe about yourself and what you are capable of. Therein lies the fun roller coaster!

You must keep living and tackling each day as it comes. Do not allow *the system* to drag you down, but instead, maintain control over your life and your approach to each new day as you work through this life challenge. You must be proactive with your health, your time, and your money—this is your life!

Can you get out your laptop or paper and pen and begin searching your personal history, and jot down what you have said and done on the good days that helped you? Can you also begin making a list of things you did and said that helped prolong a bad day? Here are some things on my list:

Litigation Story

Good Days:	Bad Days:
Got out of bed	Stayed in bed
Showered	Stayed in pajamas
Rested when I needed to	Moved from bed to couch
Ate meals at a table	Ate all day in the rediner
Listened to some great teachings	Watched things on TV that brought me lower
Encouraged someone else	Stayed in my pity party
Got some exercise	Avoided all exercise
Enjoyed the physical touch of my spouse	Forget it!
Tried to avoid negative talking	Sandblasted my family with negative mouth
Chatted with a friend that always lifts me up and re-sets me down the right path	Nobody wanted to be around me because I made them miserable too
Ate something I really love!	Just continued eating all day
Surrounded myself with uplifting music all day Engaged in a good book for short periods at a time, stretching and walking in-between	Stayed in front of TV watching shows that dragged me lower It hurts to hold a book up, so didn't really give it a good up-and-down try

CHAPTER 15

Keep Living

The world has never created a lasting pleasure.

Life can be extremely difficult when you are mourning the loss of parts of your life and freedom, grieving the loss of ability, the struggles to adapt, adjust, and make modifications to home, work, sleep, activities, hobbies, chores, housework, and so on. You must keep living!

When you are feeling down or anxious, don't keep it to yourself. One of the best ways to battle it is to talk about it. If you can, it is helpful to talk about the accident/injury and your feelings and what you are experiencing with the people you trust—family, or friends. Talking to a spiritual mentor or someone you trust can help you find new ways to deal with things that may be bothering you. Always remember that you can talk to your health-care team (your doctor, nurse, qualified counselor, or social worker). They can help you get the support you need.

I know how hard it can be to even get out of bed some mornings. Believe me, I know. I have discovered that I must set my attitude right even before I get out of bed, or while I'm in the shower, which will set the course for my day. Make a plan that does not include an exit. Drag yourself out of bed, jump in the shower and loosen those muscles up, revive all your mucous membranes, and make your body come alive. If humming, singing, or whistling helps, do it. Get ready for your day! For me personally, I have learned that if I fix myself up in the morning, even just a little, it makes me feel better all day. Yes, it may be vain, but how many mirrors do you have in your house?

Litigation Story

You can talk yourself out of stuff, and you can talk yourself into stuff. That is how our minds work. Work it to your advantage. Try your best to go to your important events and make any changes or modifications you need to and make no apologies for them. I found out I can attend more sporting events if I get up and move, walk around and stretch for a bit every chance I get, and perhaps get some fresh, buttery wonderful popcorn or a cheap hot dog to make me extremely happy. I try to apply the same approach to all sit-down events; move around when you can—stretch, readjust, whatever is necessary. Do what you must and don't feel like you must explain anything to anyone. It's nobody's business but yours.

I can so easily talk myself out of getting out of bed, or going to work, or taking a shower, or exercising, or dragging myself away from the TV, or walking around with a dust rag, or anything else. I have discovered, also, that it is just as easy to talk myself into it, and I almost always feel better when I've decided to do it. I seldom regret it.

Taking care of yourself even when you are feeling down or anxious is vital. Do your best to eat balanced meals. Try to eat what you are supposed to eat—those foods that will make you healthy and strong. If you are trying to eat healthy and stay active, those unhealthy things you love sometimes won't hurt you. Get plenty of sleep and try to get all the rest your body needs. I learned the hard way about resting when I need to rest and throwing away my pride. It is very liberating to be free from concern about how people view me physically or how they perceive my physical activity, or opinions regarding how young or how old I look. There is always a price to pay for continually seeking others' approval. We must not be weighed down by expectations from others. People who change the world have declared independence from other people's expectations (friends and family).

Take care of your family the best way you know how, despite any pain. True discipline can mean taking care of a spouse and children regardless of how you *feel*, instead of thinking that they should be taking care of you. Do your best and expect nothing less of yourself. If you have children or grandchildren, you want to set the best example for them, don't you?

It breaks my heart to hear, "My wife left me because I'm not the man I used to be." How sad it is to hear women testify that their husband divorced them because they always refuse sex because it is *uncomfortable*. Do whatever you can to keep that marriage alive! Love is not a feeling; love

Stephanie Cousins

is an action, which always results in determined acts of self-giving. Love is the willing, joyful desire to put the welfare of others above our own.

Do not forget to move around and stretch every chance you get. If I would have been more disciplined in this starting early in my life and career, I know that my physical condition would be much better today: arthritis, stiffness, bone spurring, and chronic inflammation. Please learn from my mistakes. I would quite literally in my early career work at my typewriter, a now historic piece of furniture, for five-plus hours without taking a break or getting a drink of water. In fact, I would even challenge myself to see how long I could go without having to stand up and move around. I was quite foolish, obviously, but I didn't know any better. This was before ergonomics, carpal tunnel, posture emphasis, and. "Women, do not cross your legs." I am very thankful for all the research and studies that have been conducted in the last couple of decades regarding occupational health, safety, and welfare.

Go for walks often, if you are able, and get all the exercise you can. Some of your muscles may have some getting used to, but they will strengthen and love the oxygenation. I have found that ice and/or heat really does help my muscles and my joints *if* I combine it with rest.

In those days, the best painkiller was ice; it wasn't addictive, and it was particularly effective if you poured some whiskey over it.
—George Burns[1]

But in all sincerity, avoid alcohol, cigarettes, and drugs, if you can, since these may feel good at the time but have proven to make pain and anxiety worse. If you try to replace what you are unable to do or the empty feeling you may have inside with empty substitutes or begin overindulging in excess of pretty much *anything*, you'll be heading down a path from which it's hard to come back. During trouble, stress, anxiety, and fear, whatever you run to, whether it is food, drugs, or alcohol, will end up running you.

Let's face it. The pleasure only lasts a short time, but the consequences of discomfort, weight gain, addiction, and self-condemnation continue to gain momentum, and the value of enjoyment we used to get from something starts to decrease after a certain point. This is known as the diminishing returns phenomenon. The world has never created a lasting pleasure.

Litigation Story

> If one oversteps the bounds of moderation, the
> greatest pleasures cease to please.
> —Epictetus[2]

Instead, replace these things with your favorite hobbies and activities that help to keep your body relaxed. This is your time. Take care of yourself. You deserve it, especially after what you've been through.

Here is a quick summary of helpful reminders. Keep them close to you:

> If you take pleasure in …
> If you find it helps you to …
> If it gives you peace and relaxation to …
> If it makes you smile to …
> If it brings you joy to … fish, bake, etc.
> If others comment about your good mood, write down what has been different about you and your day.
> If you've personally noticed your better mood, take note of what you've been up to.
> If you've given up something that you truly treasured, due to work, family, time, etc., remember what it was and do it.
> Are there things you've always wanted to do? Get to it! Make a plan and set a goal.
> If you have given up sex with your spouse, remember what used to make you passionate for them, stir yourself up, and get to it. Put any feelings or excuses aside. Try with all your *try*!
> If it makes your pain feel better for a while or takes your mind off it …
> If your friend says, "Wow, you look great," what did you do different?

I know that you are on the road to recovery because you made the choice to read this book. I challenge you to pick out at least one principle in this book each day and apply it to your life. It is a new day, and you can begin a new life today. Do not wait!

CHAPTER 16

The Decision Is Yours

Sometimes the hardest thing and the right thing are the same.

Yes, pursuing a claim or a lawsuit is a big decision, but you *can* survive and thrive through the litigation process until the conclusion of your personal injury/accident or workers' compensation claim. You *can* successfully work through the legal process with all the knowledge, skills, and understanding you need, with confidence and determination, in great comfort and assurance that you possess all you need. You can take your place, stand your ground, and run your case … and not let your case run you.

There are many reasons that people give for their hesitation in pursuing a legal claim. I am quite certain that you have some of your own reservations. I would encourage you to get out a pen and some paper and begin your own list of pros and cons. When we put things down on paper, clarity begins.

Here is a short list of common reasons people give for not wanting to pursue action/litigation. I hope that it will help you to sort things out, or at least inspire you to take a good, hard look at your situation and reflect upon what matters to you most before making this critical decision.

List of common reasons

1. There is a possibility that you will walk away with absolutely nothing, after all the time and money spent. We all know people who have been through a lengthy legal process after an accident or injury, and all they got

Litigation Story

was more bills and a hatred for the justice system. But on the other hand, some matters are resolved swiftly. We just don't always hear about those.

2. It is scary and stressful. Yes, indeed. But of the hundreds and hundreds of depositions and hearings I have reported, I've never seen a person testifying die from fear, pass out, or even freeze up (like you see on TV). This book you hold, and a good attorney, will have you well-prepared every step of the way.

3. It is not just business, but it is deeply personal. It is personal, but you *are* a person that matters. There are over 7.8 billion people on the planet (December 2020), and not one of them has your fingerprints! You are unique and distinct. You matter to the world, and no one can replace you. No matter what your parents may have told you, no matter if they said you were an accident, a mistake, or a source of misery in their lives; no matter that society tells you that you are just a statistic and that your value is measured in money and buying power, productivity, or appearance, and age—none of that matters because you matter to the One who created you.

4. You may know the person who caused your injury. But if you have been injured because of another person's action or lack of action, or a company's negligence, why should you be held legally or financially responsible? According to my law dictionary, the definition of responsibility is "the obligation to answer for an act done, and to repair any injury it may have caused." Those who caused your injury should pay your medical expenses, lost wages, damages, etc., shouldn't they?

5. You have a concern that friends and family will judge you if you file a lawsuit. This is an honest concern and maybe worth pondering. Some things are hard to keep secret, but wouldn't the people who care about you want what is best for you? There is a difference between frivolous lawsuits and honest ones. A good lawyer can help you determine other options for recourse and whether legal action is even necessary.

Your matter could be simply an insurance issue, and whoever caused you harm may have insurance that precisely covers your damages. And

Stephanie Cousins

while you may care what your friends and family think, it didn't happen to them, and they have no idea what you are going through.

> Do you know the difference between major surgery and minor surgery? Major surgery is when it's done on you!
> —Kevin Turner, Strategic World Impact

Sometimes, going after an individual, company, or organization is the only way to institute changes that need to be made for the health, safety, and welfare of others. Safer automobiles, safer workplaces, face shields, machine safety guards, personal protection equipment, injury and death caused by medical malpractice, quality health care, recalling of bad medicines, advancement of science regarding asbestos, cigarette smoking, hazards of vaping, a cleaner environment, repetitive injuries and ergonomics, bad nursing home care, care of our veterans, etc., are just a few examples.

6. Litigation can be expensive. It is so true. Litigation can be very expensive, but many cases can be handled quickly and inexpensively. Sometimes, just by starting litigation, the other side will be convinced that you are serious and try to reach a settlement quickly.

Often in personal injury cases, the plaintiff's attorney (the lawyer for the injured party) works on contingency, which means that he or she gets a percentage of whatever the plaintiff wins or recovers and gets nothing if the plaintiff doesn't win. In cases that are not based on contingency, typically, lawyers charge by the hour. A good lawyer will be able to give you an idea of what to expect, and it is important to review your arrangement thoroughly, including not only the per hour or percentage to be paid to an attorney, but detailed information about how the costs and expenses associated with the case are to be handled.

According to FindLaw.com, a leading provider of online legal information for consumers and small businesses, the following are the top ten reasons to hire a lawyer:

1. The law is complicated.
2. Not having a lawyer may cost you more.

Litigation Story

3. Lawyers know how to challenge evidence.
4. Filing the wrong document or following the wrong procedure could ruin your case.
5. They have access to the witnesses and experts you'll need on your side.
6. A lawyer can present your strongest case.
7. It's always better to avoid problems rather than fix them later. You may have heard the saying that "an ounce of prevention is worth a pound of cure." Well, hiring a lawyer in many instances will help you avoid potential legal headaches down the road. Do you really understand the fine print of that contract you are signing and what it will mean for you down the road? A lawyer will.
8. Lawyers know how to negotiate settlements and plea bargains. An experienced lawyer probably has seen cases similar to yours or at least knows enough to make a calculated guess about how it might get resolved at trial. Sometimes a settlement is the best choice, while other times it makes more sense to see your case through to trial. An attorney can also help negotiate a fair settlement with the opposing party.
9. The other party probably has legal representation. Nonattorneys are generally at a disadvantage when squaring off against opposing counsel or doing business with another party that has legal counsel.
10. Lawyers often provide a free consultation. Since many attorneys will meet with you for free during a face-to-face consultation, there is really no harm in talking with one. Not only will a free consultation give you an idea of the type of case you have and its likely outcome; it will help you decide whether you need to hire a lawyer.[2]

In workers' compensation matters, employers are required by law in most states to carry workers' compensation insurance to cover employees who suffer work-related injuries or illnesses. Workers' compensation claims are handled by an adjuster from the employer's insurance company. Specifically, this insurance helps pay for medical care and lost wages due to injury, disability benefits, and more.

Work-related injuries do not always occur the way we often assume,

Stephanie Cousins

like a roofer falling from a ladder or a factory worker getting his hand caught in a machine. Sometimes, people are injured when their delivery vehicle is involved in an accident or when they simply twist the wrong way when lifting. The majority of work comp depositions I have reported have involved individuals who perform the same repetitive motion daily, such as using a computer mouse or typing, grasping and using tools, and working on an assembly line. Unfortunately, other work injuries can be caused by the normal slips, trips, and falls that do so often happen.

Workers' compensation laws vary from state to state and can be extremely complicated, and it seems that very few people are aware of what constitutes a "covered" injury, what they may be entitled to, or even how to file a claim. Quite often, it appears that perhaps the employer is intentionally being elusive, nonsympathetic, or lacking any interest in helping the poor injured worker in taking the necessary steps to get help. Thus, the whole process becomes confusing and misguided, and it is easy for injured workers to fall victim to the plans and devices of employers and insurance companies, who may appear to be exerting every effort known to humankind to deny claims for coverage.

As an added caution, if you are facing retaliation for filing a lawsuit or a workers' compensation claim, if you've been fired, demoted, had your hours cut, or had to contend with any other kind of discrimination over filing a claim, you would be wise to seek representation. This is wrong and needs to stop. Unfortunately, it happens far too often. Please consider that you could play a valuable role in making sure that it doesn't happen to someone else.

If you are injured on the job site, report your injury to your employer immediately, and make sure a report is filed. Employers keep the paperwork for filing a workers' compensation claim, commonly known as an employee claim form. They may ask you to fill out the form, but it is their responsibility to report the injury to their workers' compensation insurance carrier. *Notify* your supervisor, or whoever you report to, about your injury and the way in which it occurred as soon as possible—immediately. An injured employee who fails to inform his or her employer in writing, within the required time, may lose the right to workers' compensation benefits.

You may need to consult a lawyer right away to determine what rights you have under your state's work comp laws, as each state-run

Litigation Story

program varies in what injuries and illnesses are covered and the degree of compensation and benefits. The amount that an attorney can receive for representing you also varies by state and is usually governed by state laws or regulations. In most states, the attorney will represent you on a contingency fee basis, which means the attorney will take a percentage of the amount of workers' comp benefits you receive if you win.

It breaks my heart to see injured people continue to suffer in pain needlessly while working, when they could be receiving necessary time off, rest, medical treatment, physical therapy, rehabilitation, or mental health counseling that they deserve. Do not forfeit your rights. You've earned them!

7. You believe you may be partly at fault for your own injury. You may bear some of the responsibility for what happened to you; and if that is the case, own up to it. But you can hold accountable those who also bear part of the responsibility.

> Ninety-nine percent of the failures come from
> people who have a habit of making excuses.
> —George Washington Carver[3]

8. There are things about you that you do not want other people finding out. Well, that is a legitimate concern. Some of your life that you do not want anyone finding out about may be questioned and examined if it is relevant to your case. An attentive lawyer will protect your privacy every step of the way when possible. If you have definite *skeletons in your closet*, you will want to tell your lawyer about them upfront and allow him or her the opportunity to give you an opinion on the likelihood of their importance or exposure from the other side.

9. Your personal faith or religion discourages lawsuits. It is my opinion that this is not a minor or secondary consideration. I believe that drawing upon one's faith at this critical time is essential. During our lives, we have all made a conscious decision regarding what we believe about a "higher power" or who the one true God is or isn't. I am a follower of Jesus—the Jesus of the Bible. We are a world of many religions. I believe that at this

71

Stephanie Cousins

time you will find out whether your faith system is of any value to help you, and you will find out if it has any true power at all.

It is at the very precipice of an event where your decision is made about trusting and calling upon your "higher power" with your situation, whether that situation is an accident, an injury, a bad medical report, or the hearing of bad news. I have an extra chapter in the back of this book for those that are Christian, and if you are of another faith, please simply disregard. This chapter is not for you.

10. It just doesn't seem right. For various and sundry reasons, some people just do not have a good feeling about the whole idea of becoming involved in legal matters. It is extremely important that you be fully persuaded *in your own heart* that you are doing the right thing *for you*. A trusted mentor or spiritual leader may be able to help you sort this out.

I hope this book has encouraged you to seek out wisdom while you wrestle with your decision regarding filing a claim or pursuing litigation. I firmly believe that legal recourse is right if carried out with right motives and a sincere heart: for the sake of justice, for the good of many, for protection of rights, for prevention of negligence, for protection against harassment and discrimination, and for all rights and privileges that our great Constitution affords us. I am very thankful for the justice system of America and the lawyers of America who defend those of us who cannot defend ourselves.

Unfortunately, because there are frivolous and ridiculous lawsuits filed every day in America, and people in general are often called sue-happy, this has caused many injured people to forfeit their right to legitimate recovery. Of course, there are countless answers to the question of, "Why not file a claim/lawsuit?", but your own personal reasons for hesitation are extremely important. You were injured, and you are entitled to your feelings and opinions. I would highly encourage you to seek out a trusted friend, or your spouse if you are married, to bounce things off of. They should know you best, and they may help to draw out your real feelings. Please do not keep everything bottled up inside. That can be torture!

Your accident or injury caused you trauma and pain, both physical and emotional, and has impacted your life in a multitude of ways. People can

Litigation Story

tell you all they want that they understand what you are going through, but do they really? There is one thing I do know, and that is that God alone understands you *completely*, and He is the only one that can truly turn things around for you, change your life, heal your whole person, and set you in a new direction for your life here on this earth and for eternity.

Maybe you blame God, or maybe you don't believe in Him at all. But only the God who made you can save you and help you to begin a new life, picking up the broken pieces and putting you back together even better than you were before. No matter if the court's ruling is for the plaintiff (you) or the defendant (other side), God's verdict remains unchanged:

> For God so loved the world that He gave His only begotten Son, that whoever believes in Him should not perish but have everlasting life. (John 3:16 KJV)

> Behold, I [Jesus] stand at the door and knock. If anyone hears my voice and opens the door, I will come in to him and eat with him, and he with me. (Revelation 3:20 KJV)

CHAPTER 17

What Does the Bible Say?

You keep track of all my sorrows. You have collected all my tears
in your bottle. You have recorded each one in your book.
—Psalm 56:8 (NLT)

Does the Bible illustrate how to behave during your litigation process, your deposition, hearing, or trial? Oh, if only we had an example of how to behave during legal proceedings!

Jesus Christ himself left us an amazing example to follow before, during, and after his trial, and the steps to take during persecution and prosecution. He prayed and asked his friends to pray; he faithfully treated those in authority and power respectfully, whether or not the office of those in government deserved it; he always forgave; he continually kept walking forward in faith no matter what; and he took communion. We can and must walk in Jesus's steps.

Because you are a follower of Christ, you have amazing and free access to the president of the power and light company that the rest of the world does not have. First Corinthians 2:14 says that the person without the Spirit does not accept the things that come from the Spirit of God, but considers them foolishness, and cannot understand them because they are discerned only through the Spirit.

The Bible tells us that as a believer, the Lord is on your side, which gives you a supernatural leg-up in life and in the courtroom. While this is always true, we must bear in mind, also, that there are consequences to our actions. "My conscience is clear, but that does not make me innocent. It is the Lord who judges me" (1 Corinthians 4:4).

Litigation Story

We have untapped power and resources on the ready every day of our lives. His supply is abundant and endless. He never sleeps or slumbers. So as a believer, we have 24/7 access. How great is our God!

Titus 2:6–8 instructs us to "encourage the young men to be self-controlled. In everything set them an example by doing what is good. In your teaching show integrity, seriousness and soundness of speech that cannot be condemned, so that those who oppose you may be ashamed because they have nothing bad to say about us."

In Lamentations 3:58–59 (NKJV), Jeremiah trusted God to plead his case and help him face his accusers: "Oh, Lord, You have pleaded the case for my soul; You have redeemed my life. Oh, Lord, You have seen how I am wronged; judge my case."

Because I am a Christian, a follower of Jesus, I have included this chapter for fellow believers. Let's face it. We have access to so much more that our heavenly Father wants to give us, and if ever there was a time to cry out to the One who created you, it is now. It's during our most severe trials that we are faced with the personal question, "Do I truly believe what the Bible says, or am I all talk? Do I really live what I believe?" It is rubber meets the road time.

I said earlier that I am learning more each day, through trial and error and many painful mistakes along the way. I would like to share more with you because you are also a follower of Christ. Even as I write them, I am impacted by memories of the moment of revelation of each one, and I am so thankful. The preface says that this book will help you to walk through the litigation process peacefully and victoriously. Victory does not always mean winning your case. A victory can also be the result of losing your case. What do I mean by that?

During the process, you have successfully set a Christlike example to the onlookers who were waiting to see if you would fall. Instead of giving up on your faith and hope, you have done just the opposite—drawn closer to God. What a great testimony you have. As it turns out, you are the real deal. You did survive and thrive.

Your greatest days are still ahead of you, not behind you. God has a purpose and a plan for your life that has not been rescinded, revoked, forfeited, or taken away. Your destiny predates your birth, and the Lord rejoices over you with singing (Zephaniah 3:17). Never forget who you

Stephanie Cousins

are. You are a child of the living God, and you have a purpose in this life. "Yet to all who did receive him, to those who believed in his name, he gave the right to become children of God—children born not of natural descent, nor of human decision or a husband's will, but born of God." (John 1:12–13).

The Bible says that He chose us in Him before the creation of the world, and that all our days were ordained for us before one of them came to be. In Jeremiah 1:5, God told Jeremiah, "Before I formed you in the womb, I knew you." Think about that spark of light that scientists have observed under the microscope when actual conception happens that science cannot explain. How marvelous are His works! You are one of His works.

Even though there were many ups and downs, highs and lows, times when you were proud of yourself and times when you were feeling sorry for yourself, you did hold yourself together and your life is still intact. Some people will even say that the litigation process and all that it put them through strengthened their relationships with spouses, children, and friends. Some people find an alternative career (and/or friends) better than what they gave up, with more purpose and meaning and money. Multitudes experience personal growth at a level they would not have otherwise attained.

In cooperation with your heavenly Father, you can establish your victory. You cannot blame your spouse, your lawyer, the judge or jury, the company, the negligent driver, the wet grocery store floor, or genetics. You are the only one who can make *you* the winner. Even if the whole world lets you down, you can still say, "Jesus loves me; this I know."

There's a quote I often chuckle to myself about, and for the life of me, I can't remember where I heard it: "The only way we know if we believe something is if we're doing it." Since I started writing this book, I have frequently caught myself reverting to old habits and old thinking patterns, and then I remind myself, "Please, practice what you preach!" Otherwise, you are a terrible hypocrite and of no use to anyone. It can be extremely difficult to break free from the old self, but so what? The old self was difficult too.

Litigation Story

> Look at a man in the midst of doubt and danger and you
> will learn in his hour of adversity what he really is.
> —Lucretius[1]

By no means do I have it all figured out. Because we live in a fallen world, the daily growing up never ends, but that is the fun and exciting part. We are continually, day by day, being transformed into the image of Jesus Christ. Sometimes it feels like slow motion, and sometimes it feels like drinking out of a fire hydrant. My passion and desire for an adventurous, exploratory, prove-it-to-myself approach to life is because, like everyone else, I'm prewired to come to the same empty default apart from our heavenly Father; and that is because from all of life's experiences, no matter what age or station in life, anything less than *everything* is not enough. He created us this way, so that we would seek Him and find Him, and seek Him and find Him every day. My earnest daily petition to God is, "All that I want is *everything* you have." It's a love affair that is never boring.

I also can make a choice about whether I read my Bible or whether I read something else that is not profitable for me. The apostle Paul said that "everything is permissible for the believer, but not everything is beneficial" (1 Corinthians 6:12). I know that once I have chosen to read my Bible, I've never regretted it. I have never said, "Wow, I wish I wouldn't have done that." It is living and active, sharper than any double-edged sword, penetrating even to dividing soul and spirit, joints and marrow, and judges the thoughts and attitudes of the heart. It is water to my soul. It does God no favors if I study His Word, but it does great things for me.

I'm fully convinced that if I had lived my life separated from Him and tried to do it on my own, that I would have quit working years ago, possibly living in poverty, I would have long given up on my marriage if my husband hadn't kicked me out first, quite possibly living my life in that space between my bed and my sofa, forty pounds overweight, haggard-looking, living in self-sympathy and isolation, mean and bitter. To some, this may sound like an exaggeration, but I don't mind.

Fasting has also been an especially important key for me at times when I have needed extreme clarity from God or when I've taken a nosedive and needed to reset my focus. For short periods or long periods, the lifetime benefits of hearing from God and learning during times of fasting can be

Stephanie Cousins

priceless. Things that money cannot buy. If there is something you need to get rid of in your life, try fasting for a breakthrough. Jonah 2:8 (NASB) says, "Those who cling to worthless idols forfeit the grace that could be theirs." I don't want to forfeit anything. Do you?

It has been a long and rough journey, but God does not waste a drop of sweat, and He knows every tear you've cried and uses it all for His glory. That does not mean our struggles aren't real. But He will not waste what you are going through, and the Bible says that you will reap the benefits of your adversity.

When you have been through what you've been through, you are in a perfect position to help others. You have something inside of you that most people are trying to buy over the counter. Everything God gives you, even your suffering, He gives you with someone else in mind. I have learned that part of the cure for minimizing pain is to focus on something else. Even focusing on someone else. Isaiah 58:10 says, "If you spend yourselves in behalf of the hungry and satisfy the needs of the oppressed, then your light will rise in the darkness, and your night will become like the noonday."

To continue working, despite pain, may be the wisest decision I have ever made. It has also been a daily decision. I have failed at this more times than I can even mention; but as I began to push through the best I could, I found that those daily decisions became easier and easier. I am blessed to love my work, despite pain.

Genesis 2:15 says that the Lord God took Adam and put him in the Garden of Eden to *work* it and take care of it (cultivate). Cultivation involves both creativity and effort. Work is not a curse but a great blessing. It is God who created us to work. The apostle Paul told us, "Whatever you do, work it with all your heart, as working for the Lord, not for human masters," in Colossians 3:23.

Martin Luther's doctrine of vocation: "The purpose of every vocation is to love and serve our neighbors. God does not need our good works, but our neighbor does.[2]

The following scriptures are immensely helpful when working with pain that has taken its daily toll. We must go beyond just reading them. We must meditate on them, pray to the Lord about them specifically for ourselves, and apply them, or they are of no value at all.

Litigation Story

I can do all things through Christ who strengthens me. (Philippians 4:13 NKJV)

For I know the plans I have for you, declares the Lord, plans to prosper you and not to harm you, plans to give you hope and a future. (Jeremiah 29:11)

Beloved, I pray that in all respects you may prosper and be in good health, just as your soul prospers. (3 John 2 NASB)

Those who work their land will have abundant food, but those who chase fantasies have no sense. (Proverbs 12:11 NLT)

A sluggard's appetite is never filled, but the desires of the diligent are fully satisfied. (Proverbs 13:4)

Whatever your hand finds to do, do it with all your might. (Ecclesiastes 9:10)

Diligent hands will rule, but laziness ends in forced labor. (Proverbs 12:24)

All hard work brings a profit, but mere talk leads only to poverty. (Proverbs 14:23)

Commit to the Lord whatever you do, and he will establish your plans. (Proverbs 16:3)

May the favor of the Lord our God rest on us; establish the work of our hands for us—yes, establish the work of our hands. (Psalm 90:17)

Sow your seed in the morning, and at evening let your hands not be idle, for you do not know which will succeed,

Stephanie Cousins

> whether this or that, or whether both will do equally well. (Ecclesiastes 11:6)
>
> A person can do nothing better than to eat and drink and find satisfaction in their own toil. This too, I see, is from the hand of God, for without him, who can eat or find enjoyment? (Ecclesiastes 2:24–25)
>
> Moreover, when God gives someone wealth and possessions, and the ability to enjoy them, to accept their lot and be happy in their toil—this is a gift of God. (Ecclesiastes 5:19)

Please, whatever you do, do not be too harsh on yourself or beat yourself up when you stumble. His strength is truly made perfect in our weakness. The Lord understands your heart, and He knows your thoughts whether you speak them out loud or not. And it is entirely OK to be angry at God for a time. This is normal. He is big enough to handle it. The isolation of trauma may at times seem even harder when we know there is a God who could bring resolution to our pain but doesn't. Just make sure you are talking to Him about it, so that those thoughts are discussed and healed. I always find comfort and amazement during times of questioning in Job 38–42.

It is impossible for anyone to know all the reasons why God allowed our suffering. The Bible says right now that we see only dimly as in a mirror; but when He comes, we shall see face to face. We now know in part, but then we shall know fully, even as we are fully known. John Calvin wrote about his pain: "I leave these wounds untouched, because they appear to me incurable until the Lord apply his hand."[3]

Please write me and let me know how you turned your trauma into victory.

NOTES

Chapter 1

1   "Quote by Abraham Lincoln: 'Discourage Litigation. Persuade Your Neighbors …,'" Goodreads, accessed March 6, 2021, https://www.goodreads.com/quotes/64491-discourage-litigation-persuade-your-neighbors-to-compromise-whenever-you-can.

Chapter 3

1   "Quote by Germany Kent: 'Whether You Choose to Move on from Your Struggle …,'" Goodreads, accessed March 6, 2021, http://www.goodreads.com/quotes/8401165-whether-you-choose-to-move-on-from-your-struggles-and.

Chapter 4

1   "Driving Statistics: The Ultimate List of Car Accident Statistics [2021]," Free Driving Test Practice: Driver's License Test Prep 2021, accessed March 6, 2021, https://driving-tests.org/driving-statistics/.

2   "National Safety Council," National Safety Council—Save Lives, from the Workplace to Anyplace, accessed March 6, 2021, https://www.nsc.org/work-safety/tools-resources/infographics/workplace-injuries.

Chapter 5

1   "Voltaire: I Was Never Ruined but Twice: Once When I Lost a Lawsuit, and Once When I Won One," Quotes.Net, accessed March 6, 2021, https://www.quotes.net/quote/34971.

2   "Quote by Theodore Roosevelt: 'Nothing in the World Is Worth Having or Worth d …,'" Goodreads, accessed March 6, 2021, https://www.goodreads.com/quotes/312751-nothing-in-the-world-is-worth-having-or-worth-doing.

3   Martin E. P. Seligham, *Learned Optimism* (New York: Vintage, 2006).

4   "Abraham Lincoln—Most Folks Are as Happy as They Make Up …" BrainyQuote, accessed March 6, 2021, https://www.brainyquote.com/quotes/abraham_lincoln_100845.

Chapter 6

1   "Jean de La Bruyere—Avoid Lawsuits beyond All Things …," BrainyQuote, accessed March 6, 2021, https://www.brainyquote.com/quotes/jean_de_la_bruyere_151275.

2   "Five Ways to Keep Disputes Out of Court," *Harvard Business Review*, January 1, 1990, https://hbr.org/1990/01/five-ways-to-keep-disputes-out-of-court.

Chapter 7

1   "Epictetus Quotes", BrainyQuote, accessed April 8, 2021, https://www.brainyquote.com/quotes/epictetus_149126.

2   "The Deadly Consequences of Unforgiveness," CBN News, June 22, 2015, https://www1.cbn.com/cbnnews/healthscience/2015/june/the-deadly-consequences-of-unforgiveness.

3   "Forgiveness: Your Health Depends on It," Johns Hopkins Medicine, accessed March 6, 2021, https://www.hopkinsmedicine.org/health/wellness-and-prevention/forgiveness-your-health-depends-on-it.

4   "Forgiveness: Your Health."

5   Pin on Love Quotes," Pinterest, January 17, 2012, https://www.pinterest.ca/amp/pin/472033604669416105.

6   Staff, "Kobe's Lasting Impact: 20 of Kobe Bryant's Best Quotes," NBA CA, January 26, 2021, https://ca.nba.com/news/kobes-lasting-impact-20-of-kobe-bryants-best-quotes/1e954gqpjwh1z1oosu7vm70jx1.

Chapter 8

1   "Mission & History," The American Association for Justice Archive, February 26, 2014, https://archive.justice.org/who-we-are/mission-history.

2   "Annual 2019: ABA Releases New Report on Legal Profession Statistics, Trends," American Bar Association, accessed March 6, 2021, https://www.americanbar.org/news/abanews/aba-news-archives/2019/08/annual-2019--aba-releases-new-report-on-legal-profession-statist/.

3   "Quote by Robert Frost: 'A Jury Consists of Twelve Persons Chosen to …,'" Goodreads, accessed March 6, 2021, http://goodreads.com/quotes/100333-a-jury-consists-of-twelve-persons-chosen-to-decide-who.

Chapter 10

1   "Dale Carnegie—If You Can't Sleep, Then Get up and Do …," BrainyQuote, accessed March 6, 2021, https://www.brainyquote.com/quotes/dale_carnegie_107825.

2   "Woody Allen—I'm Not Afraid to Die, I Just Don't Want To …" BrainyQuote, accessed March 6, 2021, https://www.brainyquote.com/quotes/woody_allen_148186.

3   Quotes.Net, accessed March 6, 2021, https://www.quotes.net/collection. php?add=5956.

Chapter 11

1   "Prevalence of Chronic Pain and High-Impact Chronic Pain Among Adults— United States, 2016, Centers for Disease Control and Prevention, September 16, 2019, http://dx.doi.org/10.15585/mmwr.mm6736a2.

2   "Mark Twain—Noise Proves Nothing. Often a Hen Who Has …," BrainyQuote, accessed March 6, 2021, https://www.brainyquote.com/quotes/mark_twain_ 137901.

3   "Those Who Are Good at Making Excuses Are Seldom Good at Anything Else," Quote Investigator, accessed March 6, 2021, https://quoteinvestigator. com/2018/03/08/excuses.

4   "Man's Search for Meaning," *Psychology Today*, accessed March 6, 2021, https://www.psychologytoday.com/us/blog/hide-and-seek/201205/ mans-search-meaning.

5   Halm, Joseph, "'When You Are Alive, You Don't Give up Hope' Holocaust Survivor Tells New Orleans Audience," NOLA.com, May 24, 2017, https:// www.nola.com/archive/article_3a167ae5-5695-5783-9b45-f47695b8de5d.html.

6   "Important Quotes from Anne Frank's Diary," ThoughtCo., accessed March 6, 2021, https://www.thoughtco.com/anne-frank-quotes-1779479.

7   "Top 20 Quotes of DIET EMAN Famous Quotes and Sayings," Inspiring Quotes, accessed March 6, 2021, https://www.inspiringquotes.us/ author/3126-diet-eman.

8   "Mark Twain—Age Is an Issue of Mind over Matter. If You …," BrainyQuote, accessed March 6, 2021, https://www.brainyquote.com/quotes/mark_twain_ 103892.

9   "Chronic Pain Statistics," Pain Doctor, September 17, 2018, https://paindoctor. com/resources/chronic-pain-statistics.

10   "Maximum Medical Improvement [MMI] Law and Legal Definition," USLegal., accessed March 6, 2021, https://definitions.uslegal.com/m/ maximum-medical-improvement-mmi.

11   Jessica Chaiken, "National Rehabilitation Information Center (NARIC)," *Encyclopedia of Clinical Neuropsychology* (2018): 2351–52, http://dx.doi. org/10.1007/978-3-319-57111-9_645.

12   "Zig Ziglar—Be Grateful for What You Have and Stop …," BrainyQuote, accessed March 6, 2021, https://www.brainyquote.com/quotes/zig_ziglar_ 617796.

13   "Isaac Newton—An Object in Motion Tends to Remain In …," BrainyQuote, accessed March 6, 2021, https://www.brainyquote.com/quotes/isaac_newton_ 690206.

Chapter 12

1   "7 Inspiring Quotes from Ralph Waldo Emerson That Are Useful Today," LiveAbout, accessed March 6, 2021, https://www.liveabout.com/inspiring-quotes-from-ralph-waldo-emerson-3023307.

2   "Quote by Henry Ford: 'Whether You Think You Can, or You Think You Can't …,'" Goodreads, accessed March 6, 2021, https://www.goodreads.com/quotes/638-whether-you-think-you-can-or-you-think-you-can-t-you-re.

3   "Quote by CS Lewis: 'Humility Is Not Thinking Less of Yourself, It's …,'" Goodreads, accessed March 6, 2021, https://www.goodreads.com/quotes/7288468.

4   "Marcus Aurelius—It Is Not Death That a Man Should Fear …," BrainyQuote, accessed March 6, 2021, https://www.brainyquote.com/quotes/marcus_aurelius_148732.

Chapter 13

1   "Witness Tip: Anxiety Is the #1 Barrier Affecting Communication—Litigation Insights," Litigation Insights, October 9, 2013, http://www.litigationinsights.com/witness-preparation-2/witness-tip-anxiety-is-the-1-barrier-affecting-communication.

2   "Jim Rohn—Either You Run the Day or the Day Runs You," BrainyQuote, accessed March 6, 2021, https://www.brainyquote.com/quotes/jim_rohn_162051.

3   "One-Liners: Our Collection of the Best One-Liners | Reader's Digest," *Reader's Digest*, accessed March 6, 2021, https://www.rd.com/jokes/one-liners/page/5/.

Chapter 14

1   "Michael Jordan—I've Failed over and over and over Again …," BrainyQuote, accessed March 6, 2021, https://www.brainyquote.com/quotes/michael_jordan_167379.

Chapter 15

1   "George Burns Quote: 'In Those Days the Best Painkiller Was Ice; It Wasn't Addictive and It Was Particularly Effective If You Poured Some Whis …,'" Quotefancy, accessed March 6, 2021, https://quotefancy.com/quote/1001626/George-Burns-In-those-days-the-best-painkiller-was-ice-it-wasn-t-addictive-and-it-was.

2   "Epictetus—If One Oversteps the Bounds of Moderation, the …," BrainyQuote, accessed March 6, 2021, https://www.brainyquote.com/quotes/epictetus_397220.

Chapter 16

1   "Top Ten Reasons to Hire a Lawyer," FindLaw, accessed July 28, 2020, https://hirealawyer.findlaw.com/do-you-need-a-lawyer/top-ten-reasons-to-hire-a-lawyer.html.

2   "George Washington Carver Quotes," BrainyQuote, accessed March 6, 2021, https://www.brainyquote.com/authors/george-washington-carver-quotes.

Chapter 17

1   "QUOTE OF THE DAY: Look at a Man in the Midst of Doubt and Danger and You Will Learn in His Hour of Adversity What He Really I ..., | Quote of the Day, Quotes, Adversity," Pinterest, accessed March 6, 2021, https://www.pinterest.com/pin/455215474817988033/.

2   "Martin Luther on Vocation and Serving Our Neighbors," Acton Institute, accessed March 6, 2021, https://www.acton.org/pub/commentary/2016/03/30/martin-luther-vocation-and-serving-our-neighbors.

3   *Project Gutenberg's Letters of John Calvin*, vol. 2 of 4, ed. Jules Bonnet.

CPSIA information can be obtained
at www.ICGtesting.com
Printed in the USA
BVHW030829310721
613338BV00005B/108